First Class Delivery
A national survey of women's views of maternity care

first class
delivery

A national survey of women's views of maternity care

Jo Garcia
Maggie Redshaw
Beverley Fitzsimons
Janet Keene

AUDIT
COMMISSION
Promoting the best use of public money

National Perinatal Epidemiology Unit

© Audit Commission 1998

First published in January 1998 by the Audit Commission
for Local Authorities and the National Health Service in
England and Wales, 1 Vincent Square, London SW1P 2PN

Designed and typeset by John Miles

Printed in the UK for the Audit Commission by
Belmont Press

ISBN 186240 065 2   **04378780**

Photographs: Pictor International (cover, p75);
Sally & Richard Greenhill (pp3, 7, 33, 65, 81).

Contents

Foreword

The Audit Commission

The Audit Commission oversees the external audit of the National Health Service and Local Authorities in England and Wales. As part of this function, the Commission is required to carry out national studies of 'value for money' in different aspects of health and local government services. These studies lead to national reports and local audits of the services in question, and make recommendations for improving economy, effectiveness and efficiency. The methodology for local audits is devised by national studies' research teams. As well as value for money studies, the Commission also oversees the financial ('regularity') audit of these bodies.

The areas of focus for national studies are decided on in a number of ways. The Commission consults widely within the NHS and professional bodies for guidance on areas that would most benefit from study. On the basis of this process, maternity services were selected for review and a two-year study was undertaken in 1995-96. The main report of this study was published in March 1997. This volume provides a more detailed report of the findings of the survey of recent mothers carried out for the Audit Commission as part of the study of maternity services.

The National Perinatal Epidemiology Unit

The National Perinatal Epidemiology Unit is a multidisciplinary research unit within Oxford University. It was set up in 1978 to undertake research which is of direct relevance to pregnant women, their babies, their carers and health policymakers. It is funded by the Department of Health and also receives grants from research councils, international organisations and charities.

Acknowledgements

We are very grateful to all the women who filled in the questionnaire and went to so much trouble to record their views and experiences. Thanks also to:

Jocelyn Cornwell, Jane Laughton, Bruce Anderson, John Bailey, Kate Flannery: Audit Commission

Sally Marchant, Alison Macfarlane, Ann Quinn, Jane Henderson, Tracy Roberts, Kirstie McKenzie-McHarg, Hazel Ashurst, Sarah Ayers, Karen Gallagher, Kate Fredrick: National Perinatal Epidemiology Unit

Janet Richardson: City and Hackney Community Health Council

Verena Wallace, Jane Cowl: Changing Childbirth Team

Stephanie Brown: Centre for the Study of Mothers' and Children's Health, La Trobe University, Melbourne, Australia

Philip Steer: Chelsea and Westminster Hospital

Meg Gready: National Childbirth Trust

Colleagues at the Department of Health

Funding for the survey and analysis came from the Audit Commission. Jo Garcia is paid by the Department of Health.

The Authors

Beverley Fitzsimons is a project manager for the Audit Commission's Health and Personal Social Services Directorate.

Jo Garcia is a social scientist for the National Perinatal Epidemiology Unit, Oxford University.

Janet Keene is a researcher for the National Perinatal Epidemiology Unit, Oxford University.

Maggie Redshaw is a senior lecturer in developmental psychology, University of the West of England and Honorary Research Fellow at the Institute of Child Health, University of Bristol.

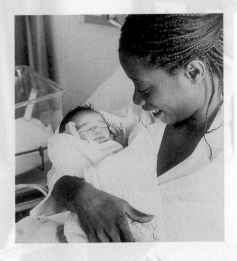

Chapter 1

The survey of recent mothers

'... while I was pregnant, from beginning to end, the staff of the hospital and doctor and the midwife of the doctor's surgery were really good. I have no complaint for anything. I am pleased to fill in this questionnaire because it will help others know how they should have been treated.'

'... so yes, my ordeal probably happens every day. Is this questionnaire really going to make a difference? I doubt it!'

This report is part of a study of maternity services carried out in England and Wales by the Audit Commission. It gives the detailed results of a large national survey of mothers who gave birth in 1995. Some of the results of the mothers' survey were published in March 1997 in the Audit Commission report *First Class Delivery*,[1] together with findings from local studies of maternity care and staff surveys. This volume allows more space to be given to women's views and experiences, and will be of interest to groups working on behalf of maternity service users, and to midwives, doctors, managers, policymakers and researchers.

Getting information about women's views and experiences is important for several reasons.

- All health care is about more than the technical aspects of treatment. People's health matters to them and they react to care as people, not just as bodies. Good care meets the needs of people as individuals, including their needs for encouragement, information and reassurance.

- Women's reactions to care around the time of birth can affect they way they care for themselves and their baby and influence the contact they go on to have with care-givers. Whether women feel that they have had a good or bad experience is partly affected by the clinical events they experience. In addition, the explanations and support they get from staff can be important to them for a long time. When things go well, women may feel more confident with the new baby and happier to ask for help and advice from care-givers. When things go badly, women may find themselves going over the events again and again in their minds and may be very anxious about another pregnancy.

- Some aspects of care can be assessed only by asking women, or are more practical to get this way. For example, if a trust aims to provide women with information about local maternity services, then it is important to ask whether women actually did receive this information. Women need to be the ones to say whether they got enough information, whether they were able to understand what was said to them, whether they were treated kindly, and whether the food and other facilities were good. Women are also best able to say whether they knew the care-givers who looked after them at different stages.

1 Audit Commission (1997) *First Class Delivery*. London.

The survey of recent mothers carried out for the Audit Commission is particularly useful because it provides national data at a crucial time for maternity care. The questionnaire allowed women to describe the care they had received, to express their views about it in structured questions and to make longer written comments if they wanted to. Some of the results are about clinical aspects of care; this is useful in giving a background to women's experiences and also because national statistics about maternity care do not cover all topics of interest.[2] This report has an appendix of detailed tables for reference.

How the survey was carried out

The questionnaire was sent to a random sample of women in England and Wales who had a baby in June and July 1995. It was sent when their babies were around four months old and covered care in pregnancy, at the birth and after (see Appendix 1 for more details). Of the 3,570 women sent a questionnaire, 2,406 women responded, giving a response rate of 67%.

How the report is organised

The main results are divided into three sections. The first (Chapter 2) is about the clinical care that women had and how it was organised. The next, and longest section (Chapter 3) is about women's views and experiences of care and includes many comments from the questionnaires. Then, lastly, there is a section about women whose baby had been cared for in a neonatal unit (Chapter 4). All the chapters start with comments from women that have been chosen to give an idea of the range of views that women have, and to make the point that their experiences of care are often very important for them and their families. Further details of the methods used in the survey and the characteristics of the women who responded are given in Appendix 1. Appendix 2 contains tables that give more detail and all the base numbers. Information about studies of women's views of care is in Appendix 3.

2 But see the most recent national data in: Department of Health (1997) *NHS Maternity Statistics, England: 1989-90 to 1994-5*. Statistical Bulletin 1997/28. London, Department of Health.

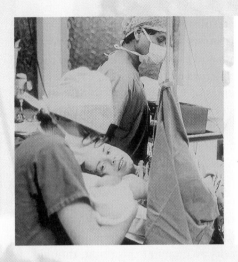

Chapter 2

The care received

'Many of the preconceived ideas I had before the birth changed due to the need for an induction and the difficult labour. Although I never wanted to be induced or have an epidural etc, I believe what was done was the best for me and the baby. The staff involved in the birth were wonderful.'

'The care I would have liked to receive would have been more home care from your community midwife before the birth of your unborn baby. To discuss a full plan about the care you wish to receive, to give you more confidence for the birth...I also think if you were to see a set of the same midwives at the hospital you would get to know them at your antenatal and that would .... make you more ready for the birth and know there is always someone there who you can talk to.'

This chapter describes the results about patterns of care, procedures and interventions from the survey of mothers. The information provides the context for women's views and experiences (covered in the next chapter) and gives an up-to-date picture of the way that care is organised, picking up some of the themes of *Changing Childbirth*.[3] It also provides some data about key aspects of clinical care such as ultrasound scans and pain relief in childbirth. The relevant tables in the Appendix give more detail and can be used for comparison with other studies.

Care in pregnancy

At the start of pregnancy, three-quarters of women went to the GP to discuss their maternity care. Nearly all the others went to see a midwife (22%). On average, women were 8 weeks pregnant at this point, though the range was very wide - over a third of women went very early (up to 6 weeks) and a small number waited until much later in pregnancy. Figure 1 shows the breakdown of results (see also Appendix Table 2.1).

Figure 1   The time of mother's first contact to discuss maternity care

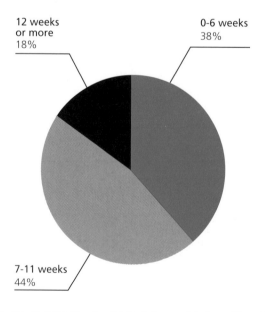

12 weeks or more 18%

0-6 weeks 38%

7-11 weeks 44%

3 Department of Health (1993) *Changing Childbirth, Report of the Expert Maternity Group*. London, HMSO.

Only one woman out of 2,406 reported in the questionnaire that she had not had any antenatal care and three answered that they could not remember. This very low figure may be a slight underestimate. In the interview survey of 1,005 women carried out in 1993 for the Expert Maternity Group,[4] 15 women (1%) reported that they had had no antenatal care in their last pregnancy. The most recent Infant Feeding survey, carried out in 1995, also shows that 1% of women had no antenatal care.[5]

Women were asked to estimate the numbers of check-ups at different locations and with different care-givers. The questions were clearly not easy to answer and often the numbers of visits that a woman had did not come to the same total when different questions were compared. Nearly half the women reported between 11 and 15 visits (Figure 2; details in Appendix Table 2.2).

Figure 2   Distribution of total number of antenatal visits (all locations)

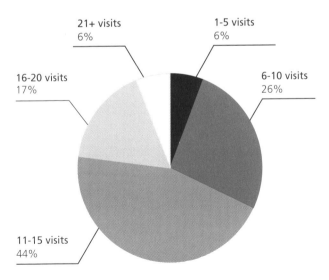

4   Rudat K, Roberts C, Chowdhury R (1993) *Maternity Services: A Comparative Survey of Afro-Caribbean, Asian and White Women Commissioned by the Expert Maternity Group.* London, MORI Health Research.
5   Foster K, Lader D, Cheesbrough S (1997) *Infant Feeding 1995.* London, the Stationery Office.

The data also show, not surprisingly, that most women had antenatal check-ups at the hospital *and* at the GP's surgery.[6] Around a third of women had some antenatal care at home; 84% had some care in hospital and 97% had some care at a GP's surgery. The 16% of women who reported no hospital antenatal care probably did have some visits to hospital; all but two of them had ultrasound scans, though they may not have had full check-ups there. Only 3% of women reported no antenatal checks at the GP's surgery.

The analysis attempted to distinguish those who had mainly hospital-based care, and those who had mainly community-based care. Two groups of women were identified: a small group who had received more antenatal check-ups in hospital than in the community (Group H) and another much larger group who had had more antenatal check-ups in the community than in hospital (Group C). Their average numbers of visits are shown in Table 1.

Table 1   Mean numbers of antenatal visits in different locations

	Mean numbers of visits in:			
	Hospital	GP's Surgery	Home	Total
Group H (318)	8	3	-	11
Group C (1,892)	3	10	1	14

Group H - women who had more visits in hospital than in community
Group C - women who had more visits in community than in hospital

Compared to Group C, women in Group H were more likely to be over 35 and under 20, to be non-white and to have had problems in a previous pregnancy. They were more likely to have had five or more scans (37% v. 9%) and to have had antenatal screening with amniocentesis or chorion villus sampling (10% v. 6%). Group H is probably a mixture of women

6   Audit Commission (1997) *First Class Delivery*, London, pp21-2.

judged to be at higher risk of complications and so referred for specialist
care, and a smaller number of women living in inner city areas whose GPs
do not provide maternity care. This latter category has become less
numerous over the last 20 years. It is striking that the women apparently at
higher risk had fewer antenatal visits.

There is some evidence of regional differences in patterns of antenatal care
(Figure 3 and Appendix Tables 2.3 and 2.4). Women living in the South
East had fewer antenatal visits in total than women in the rest of England
and Wales. Women in the South West had fewer hospital visits and more
of their care in the community. In contrast, women in Wales and the North
West had more hospital visits and a greater proportion of them had more
antenatal visits in hospital than in the community. The differences are quite
large. For example, 12% of women in the South West reported six or more
hospital antenatal visits compared to 26% in the North West and 31% in
Wales. Differences of this magnitude are unlikely to be due to variations in
clinical need, and so represent potential savings to the NHS.[7] Although

Figure 3   Total number of antenatal visits by region

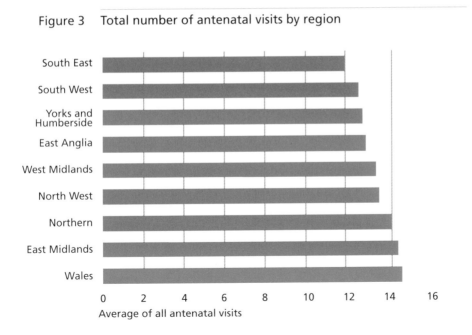

Average of all antenatal visits

7   Audit Commission (1997) *First Class Delivery*, London, pp25-7.

some studies have been carried out, further research is needed to evaluate different patterns of antenatal care using a range of methods including trials, economic assessment and clinical audit. Women's views and concerns are being included in many of these studies, and this is crucial since antenatal care has an important component of reassurance and information-giving.[8]

Antenatal screening tests

Checks on the health and well-being of pregnant women occur at different stages in pregnancy. Tests aimed at detecting possible abnormalities in the baby tend to be carried out in the first half of pregnancy, and information about what the tests involve needs to be provided to women at early antenatal visits if it is to be useful to them.

Some of the tests that can be used to assist in detecting abnormalities in the baby are offered to all women, others are used selectively. The tests available include: tests using blood samples such as the alpha-fetoprotein (AFP) test, and the double and triple tests which are carried out between 15 and 18 weeks; early ultrasound scans which measure the nuchal fold thickness; and more invasive procedures which involve taking samples of the placenta (chorion villus sampling, CVS) or samples of amniotic fluid (amniocentesis), both using ultrasound as a guide.

Fewer than 2% of the study population (40 women) had chorion villus sampling, a procedure which is usually carried out at between 8 and 12 weeks of pregnancy. More women (4.5%, 109 women) had amniocentesis, which is carried out between 14 and 18 weeks.

Women's views on why they had CVS or amniocentesis

Most of the women having these procedures felt that the reasons for doing so were clearly explained to them (35 out of 37 for CVS; 106 out of 109 for amniocentesis). When asked why they had had CVS, half of the 36 women involved said that they themselves had particularly wanted this test. Some were advised to have it because of their age (5) or their family history (2), and others gave reasons which included problems with a previous baby and concerns about possible abnormalities in the present pregnancy (6). When asked why they had had amniocentesis, a quarter of the women

---

8   Sikorski J, Wilson J, Clement S et al (1996) 'A randomised controlled trial comparing two schedules of antenatal visits: the antenatal care project', *BMJ*, Vol. 312, pp546-53.

concerned said it was routine for their age group, nearly half said they particularly wanted the test and half said it was carried out as a result of earlier blood tests. Among the 'other' reasons given were concerns arising from screening tests carried out earlier in the pregnancy (7).

Which women had CVS or amniocentesis?

As was expected, older women were significantly more likely to have these tests (Figure 4 and Appendix Table 2.5). Of all those having these procedures, more than half (56%) were aged 35 and over. As well as being older than average, those who had either of these types of invasive screening procedures may be at higher risk for other reasons. They were significantly more likely to go on to have an operative delivery of some kind: a total of 29% (41) had a caesarean section birth, and 14% (20) had either a forceps or ventouse delivery. Higher proportions of these women also had babies who were born preterm (21% compared with 12%) and admitted to neonatal care (17%, 23 out of 136, compared with 9%, 186 out of 2,015, for the rest of the study sample).

Figure 4   Age distribution of women having CVS or amniocentesis compared with the whole sample

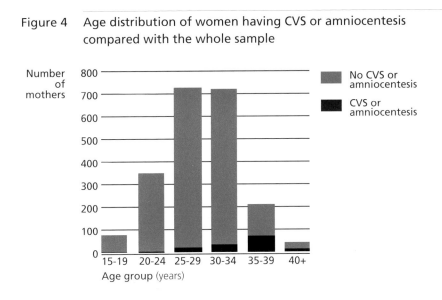

Ultrasound scans

Ultrasound scanning in pregnancy is common, but the numbers of scans that an individual woman receives is highly variable.[9] The clinical objectives in scanning the developing baby are varied, and the ways in which they are used are subject to local policies. In normal pregnancies, 'dating' scans are most often carried out late in the first trimester (three months) and 'anomaly' scans at around 18-20 weeks' gestation (some trusts routinely carry out the first or both of these for all women). Ultrasound is also used to guide the screening procedures in which samples of the amniotic fluid or placental tissues are required. Where there is concern about the growth of the baby, the location of the placenta or some other possible problem, additional scans may be carried out.

Almost all the women had scans; only five women had not and one could not remember. The remaining 99.8% had one or more scans. The first scan was done at 14 weeks of pregnancy on average, ranging from 2 to 36 weeks. (Table 2 gives the numbers at different gestations and Appendix Table 2.6 gives this information in more detail. The total numbers of scans reported by women [mean 3, median 2, range 1-20] are shown in Table 3.) The number of scans for an individual is likely to reflect local policies, the practice of particular care-givers and clinical concern based on the woman's history and symptoms. It may also reflect a woman's anxiety about her baby. On the other hand parents may want scans because they can actually see their unborn baby and often buy a photograph to take away with them.

Table 2   Timing of first scan (gestational age in weeks)

Timing of first scan	No.	%	
<12 weeks	573	24	
12-15 weeks	669	28	
16-19 weeks	835	35	
20+ weeks	290	12	
Total	2,367	100	

9   Audit Commission (1997) *First Class Delivery*, London, p28.

Table 3   Number of scans reported by women

Total No. of scans	No. of women	%	
1 scan	474	20	
2 scans	851	36	
3 scans	504	21	
4 scans	230	10	
5 scans	124	5	
6+ scans	200	8	
Total replies	2,383	100	

What factors were associated with greater numbers of scans? To answer this question, we divided the numbers of scans per woman into low, medium and high categories, and examined their relationships with other factors (see Appendix Table 2.7). Greater numbers of ultrasound scans were associated with possible indicators of clinical need, such as problems in a previous pregnancy, more nights in hospital antenatally, and higher levels of induction, continuous monitoring in labour, caesarean section and other forms of operative delivery. In addition, a high number of scans was more common in women who had CVS or amniocentesis, with nearly three-quarters (74%) having three or more scans in the course of their pregnancy and a quarter having five or more scans. Mothers having twins, going into preterm labour and having a baby who was admitted to a neonatal unit were also more likely to report a high number of scans.

Care at the birth

Almost all the women in the survey (98%) had their babies in hospital; 33 of these were in a GP unit within the hospital. Fifty had the baby at home, two in a neighbour's house, one in a GP unit separate from the hospital and two in an ambulance. Sixteen of the 52 women who had a baby at home (or a neighbour's house) had not planned to do this.

Women were asked who was with them for the birth. The full list of professionals present is given in Appendix Table 2.8, and the main combinations of care-givers are shown in Table 4. In addition, over 90% of women reported that their partner or another companion was with them during labour and birth. Just over half the women reported that the birth took place without a doctor of any kind being present. If we exclude caesarean section, the proportion rises to 63%. This allows comparison with the four local surveys carried out in 1987 to test the OPCS Survey Manual questionnaire.[10] In those surveys, the proportion of women delivering with no doctor present ranged from 52% to 76% (excluding caesarean sections).

Table 4   Which members of staff were present in the room when your baby was born?

Care-givers present:	No.	%	
Midwife (or midwives) but no doctors	1,239	54	
Midwife (or midwives) and doctor(s)	1,027	45	
Other staff combinations	28	1	
No professionals	10	-	
Sub-total	2,304	100	
Don't know or general anaesthetic	80		
Missing	22		
Total	2,406		

The data also allowed the different kinds of doctor to be distinguished from each other. Women were asked who was actively involved in the birth (see Appendix Table 2.9). A third of women reported that they delivered with an obstetrician present and in three-quarters of these cases the obstetrician was actively involved in the birth. This corresponds well with the figures for 1994-5 for England and Wales from routine data, where 28% of the reported deliveries were conducted by a doctor.[11] Paediatricians were reported by women as being there in 28% of births and, again, three-

10   Mason V (1989) *Women's Experiences of Maternity Care: A Survey Manual*. London, HMSO.
11   Department of Health (1997) *NHS Maternity Statistics, England: 1989-90 to 1994-5*. Statistical Bulletin 1997/28. London, Department of Health.

quarters were actively involved. GPs were less likely to be present than other doctors. Only 69 women (3%) said that their GP had been there for the birth. Ten women reported that they had not had a professional care-giver there for the birth because they had the baby too quickly; eight at home and two in hospital without a midwife being present. A further three women were looked after only by ambulance staff. Eighty women said that they did not know which staff had been there, mostly because they had a general anaesthetic, although nearly half of these knew of several people who were involved.

Women were asked if they had met, before the actual birth, all or some of the staff who cared for them. Forty nine percent said that they had, a higher figure than those reported in the surveys done in 1987 to test the OPCS Survey Manual questionnaire.[12] In those surveys, the proportion who had met any of the staff caring for them in labour ranged from 15% to 28% (unpublished data). The *Changing Childbirth* target is that 75% of women should know the person who cares for them during their delivery.

Half the women in the Audit Commission survey said that one midwife had been able to remain with them throughout the whole labour. Not surprisingly, this was very much affected by practical considerations; these women were likely to have had a shorter labour, a normal vaginal birth and to be having a second or subsequent baby. Women in this and other surveys feel strongly about being able to have the same staff members with them if possible.[13] For example, 48% of respondents said that it was *very important* to have the same staff throughout; in contrast, only 24% said that it was *very important* to have met the staff before. It may be possible to find practical ways to increase the proportion of women cared for by the same midwife throughout labour and birth.[14] Local audits looking at staff shift patterns could be useful here.

12   Mason V (1989) *Women's Experience of Maternity Care: A Survey Manual*. London, HMSO.

13   Garcia J (1995) 'Continuity of carer in context: what matters to women?' in Page L (ed) *Effective Group Practice in Midwifery*. Oxford, Blackwell Scientific.

14   Audit Commission (1997) *First Class Delivery*, London, pp38-40.

Table 5 shows women's reports of the total number of midwives caring for them in labour and for the birth. Over a third of women were cared for by three or more midwives.

Table 5   The reported number of midwives caring for women in labour

	No.	%	
One	553	24	
Two	955	41	
Three	472	20	
Four or more	332	14	
Total	2,312	100	

Induction and augmentation

Induction of labour can take different forms: these include the use of drugs to stimulate labour and artificial rupture of membranes (ARM). These techniques may be used separately and at different points during the same labour. Mothers in the study were asked about induction in general terms, and also about whether their labour was 'speeded up' or augmented.

Altogether 65% of women reported that they had started labour spontaneously. A total of 26% were induced and 8% had a planned caesarean and did not go into labour at all. A substantial number of women (52% excluding those who did not labour) reported that their labour had been augmented and nearly half of these (47%) had labours that were augmented following initial induction. It is difficult to compare these figures for induction and augmentation of labour with those from other studies, or from national statistics, because the questions are not always put in the same way. In *Home Births*, a large study done in 1994 which compared the experience of low risk women who delivered in hospital or at home,[15] 19% of the women who gave birth in hospital were reported to have been induced. This figure is lower than that found in the Audit Commission Survey, but the *Home Births* study women were selected to be comparable in 'risk' to those booked for a home birth. There is no

15 Chamberlain G, Wraight A, Crowley P (eds) (1996) *Home Births*. London, Parthenon.

professional consensus about appropriate levels of induction and augmentation of labour, but rates do vary between trusts in other studies. This may be a topic where audit should be considered.

The reasons given for induction are shown in Table 6. Being overdue was the most common reason, followed by staff concerns about the woman's own or her baby's health. Among the 'other' reasons given were prolonged rupture of membranes (17), the size of the baby (8) and an adverse obstetric history, sometimes involving previous pregnancy losses (7). Two women reported that they had been induced so that their husbands, who were working abroad or in the forces, would not miss the birth.

Table 6   Reasons given by women for labour being induced (n=625) (more than one reason might apply)

Reported reasons for induction	No.	%	
Baby overdue	285	46	
Concerns about the baby	191	31	
Concerns about the mother	155	25	
Contractions started and stopped	106	17	
Other reason	54	9	

Monitoring during labour

A range of methods are used to monitor babies' well-being and responses to the events during labour, mainly measuring the fetal heart rate and uterine contractions. Fetal heart-rate monitoring can be carried out at intervals or to provide a continuous record. Some procedures are more invasive than others. Those that are intermittent obviously allow for greater mobility and changes of position. Different types of monitoring may be used depending on hospital policy, the equipment available, the wishes of the women concerned and the clinical needs of the situation. Also, different methods are likely to be used at different points in labour. The methods reported by the women in the survey are listed in Table 7. Altogether, for women who did not have a planned caesarean, electronic fetal monitoring was used in 87% of labours and was continuous in 53%.

Table 7   Types of intrapartum monitoring reported (n= 2,192) (excluding women who did not go into labour)

Method of monitoring (women could tick more than one)

	No.	%	
Stethoscope or ear trumpet intermittently	335	15	▬▬
Sonicaid hand-held monitor used intermittently	370	17	▬▬
A monitor and belt around the abdomen used intermittently	904	41	▬▬▬▬▬
A monitor and belt used constantly	1,022	47	▬▬▬▬▬▬
Constant monitoring with a clip attached to the baby's scalp	383	18	▬▬
None of these	64	3	▮

Pain relief

Pain relief in labour, like methods of induction, can take very different forms, some of which can be used at different stages in the birth process. As labour progresses and the kind of intervention needed changes, other types of pain relief may be offered or chosen. In general, women are more likely to use natural and other less invasive techniques during early labour, and to request analgesia as they experience more painful contractions. The women in the study were asked about the use of natural methods such as relaxation techniques but also about the use of pethidine and epidural anaesthesia (Table 8). Gas and air (entonox) by face mask was most often reported, followed by pethidine (or a similar injection). Next came epidural (or spinal) analgesia. However, these were not used exclusively: some women, for example, at different points in their labour, reported being given both pethidine and epidural analgesia (10%, 221).

The figures here for the percentages of women reporting the use of entonox, pethidine and epidural are very similar to those found in the 1995 *Infant Feeding* survey, using a somewhat different question.[16]

16   Foster K, Lader D, Cheesbrough S. (1997) *Infant Feeding 1995*. London, the Stationery Office. This study found that entonox had been used by 71%, pethidine by 42% and epidural by 28%.

Table 8   Methods of relieving pain in labour reported by women
(base = 2,175)

(adds to more than 100%. Those who had a planned caesarean section
and who did not go into labour are not included)

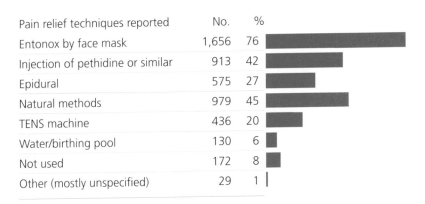

Pain relief techniques reported	No.	%
Entonox by face mask	1,656	76
Injection of pethidine or similar	913	42
Epidural	575	27
Natural methods	979	45
TENS machine	436	20
Water/birthing pool	130	6
Not used	172	8
Other (mostly unspecified)	29	1

The proportion reporting epidural analgesia is somewhat higher than the
most recent figure from national data (21% in England and Wales in 1994-
5).[17] In the Audit Commission survey there were some differences in the use
of epidural, depending on the region where the woman lived, though these
were not as big as some of the other regional differences found. Other
studies have shown that epidural use varies a lot between hospitals partly
because it depends on access to anaesthetists.[18]

Type of delivery

Of the women surveyed, more than two-thirds (71%) reported a normal
vaginal delivery.[19] A further 12% had assisted vaginal deliveries, with
slightly more of these involving the use of forceps (6.2%) than ventouse
(vacuum extraction) (5.4%). On the present evidence, the use of ventouse
is recommended where possible for assisted vaginal births because it leads
to less trauma for the mother.[20] The use of the ventouse is increasing, but

17 Department of Health (1997) NHS Maternity Statistics, England: 1989-90 to 1994-5. Statistical Bulletin
    1997/28. London, Department of Health.
18 Gready M, Newburn M, Dodds R, Gauge S (1995) Birth Choices: Women's Expectations and Experiences.
    London, National Childbirth Trust. Audit Commission (1997) First Class Delivery, p36. Audit Commission
    (1997) Anaesthesia Under Examination. London.
19 Audit Commission (1997) First Class Delivery, London, p43.
20 Benbow A, Semple D, Maresh M (1997) Effective Procedures Suitable for Audit. Manchester, Royal College of
    Obstetricians and Gynaecologists Clinical Audit Unit.

further progress is necessary to meet the recommendations. The caesarean section rate (at 17%) was a little higher than the most recent national rate (15% in 1994-5) available from routine data.[21] There were slightly more emergency caesarean sections reported than planned. Of the women having caesarean sections, more than two-thirds had it carried out under epidural analgesia (69%, 288 women) and were thus conscious when their baby was born. Some of the factors associated with the different types of delivery are shown in Appendix Table 2.10.

The reasons the women gave for giving birth by caesarean section were varied and differed according to whether the procedure was planned or not (Figure 5 and Appendix Table 2.11). Emergency caesareans were more likely to take place:

- where the baby was distressed,

- the labour was preterm,

- or twins were to be delivered.

Figure 5   Reasons for having a caesarean section
Comparison of planned and emergency caesarean deliveries
(more than one reason could be given)

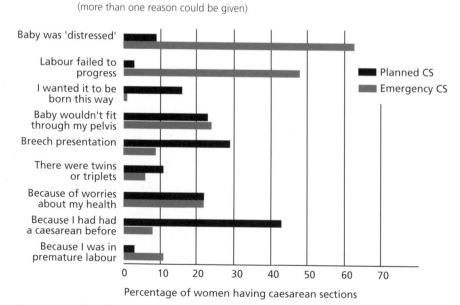

Percentage of women having caesarean sections

21 Department of Health (1997) NHS Maternity Statistics, England: 1989-90 to 1994-5. Statistical Bulletin 1997/28. London, Department of Health.

Planned caesareans were more likely:

• when mothers had given birth in this way before,

• where infants were presenting as a breech, and

• if mothers did not want a vaginal delivery.

Caesarean sections, for reasons of maternal health or cephalo-pelvic disproportion were equally likely to be planned or emergency procedures. It is recommended that previous caesarean section should not routinely be considered a reason for a caesarean birth.[22]

Position at delivery

The position that women adopt in giving birth is influenced by a multiplicity of factors, individual choice and clinical need among them. The positions reported by the women in the sample are shown in Figure 6 and Appendix Table 2.12. The women who were lying flat or supported by

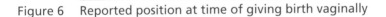

Figure 6   Reported position at time of giving birth vaginally

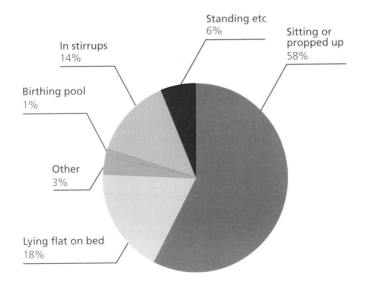

Standing etc
6%

Sitting or
propped up
58%

In stirrups
14%

Birthing pool
1%

Other
3%

Lying flat on bed
18%

22 Benbow A, Semple D, Maresh M (1997) *Effective Procedures Suitable for Audit*. Manchester, Royal College of Obstetricians and Gynaecologists Clinical Audit Unit.

stirrups included more women having assisted deliveries. Only 4% of women having a normal vaginal birth used stirrups.

A majority of women (73%) felt that they would *not* have liked to try another position for the birth. The remainder (19%) would possibly have liked to try another position and 6% would definitely have preferred an alternative. It would be interesting to know whether women are adopting more varied positions for delivery than they did in the past. Unfortunately questions about this have not been asked in comparable ways in different surveys. In the *Home Births* study,[23] women having a baby at home were much more likely to give birth squatting, kneeling or on all fours than comparable women having a baby in hospital (37% v. 6%).

Episiotomy

For the study population having a vaginal (non-caesarean) delivery, the episiotomy rate was 28%.[24] Episiotomy was more common for women whose babies were delivered by forceps or ventouse, and for women having their first baby, regardless of type of delivery (see Table 9).[25] The rates were similar across the age groups examined. There were differences in the proportion of episiotomies depending on the region where the woman lived. For example, women from the east or west Midlands were more than twice as likely to report an episiotomy than women from Wales or the south-west of England (Appendix Table 2.13). This suggests that local audits of the use of episiotomy would be worthwhile.

Table 9   Episiotomy rates in relation to type of delivery and whether baby was first or subsequent (546 episiotomies, 1,951 births).

Type of delivery	First birth %	Subsequent birth %
Normal vaginal delivery	30	13
Forceps and ventouse	86	73

23 Chamberlain G, Wraight A, Crowley P (eds) (1996) *Home Births*. London, Parthenon.
24 Graham I (1997) *Episiotomy: Challenging Obstetric Intervention*. Oxford, Blackwell Scientific. *First Class Delivery*, p45.
25 See also the analysis in: Department of Health (1997) *NHS Maternity Statistics, England: 1989-90 to 1994-5*. Statistical Bulletin 1997/28. London, Department of Health.

Women were asked why the episiotomy had been carried out. The reasons most commonly given were to facilitate a quicker and easier delivery of the baby and to avoid a perineal tear (Table 10). In just over a third of women, the fact that the baby was distressed was also mentioned as a factor. Other reasons included episiotomy being used to facilitate an instrumental delivery and to assist the delivery of a baby who was presenting awkwardly.

Table 10   Reasons reported for episiotomy (more than one reason could be given) (n=545)

Reasons	No.	%	
Easier and quicker delivery	369	68	
To avoid a tear	227	42	
Baby was 'distressed'	199	37	
What woman wanted	16	3	
Other	45	8	

Of those women who had had a vaginal birth, 57% reported that they had stitches - 28% following an episiotomy and 29% for a tear. Others may have had unsutured tears, but this was not asked about. For a large proportion of these women (47%), the repair took place straight away, though for more than half there was some delay (Table 11).

Table 11   Reported timing of perineal repair following delivery

Timing of repair	No.	%	
Straight away	521	47	
Within 20 minutes	341	31	
20-60 minutes	154	14	
More than an hour after delivery	92	8	
Total	1,108	100	

Women in this survey were less likely to report an episiotomy than women in some earlier studies. For example, in the four local surveys carried out in 1987 to test the OPCS Survey Manual questionnaire,[26] women with vaginal births reported episiotomy rates at or over 40% in three out of the four test districts; at least two-thirds of women had stitches (unpublished data). National data also show a striking fall in the episiotomy rate since 1980.[27]

Hospital care after the birth

Altogether 98% of women had a stay in hospital after the birth (including 10 who went in after a birth at home). The figures indicate somewhat longer stays than expected on the basis of national data [28](Table 12). Short stays were less common in the north of England than in other regions[29] (Figure 7 and Appendix Table 2.14).

Table 12   Length of stay in hospital after the birth

	No.	%	
less than 6 hours	76	3	▮
>6 but <24 hours	449	19	▆
1-2 days	730	31	▆
3-5 days	821	35	▆
6 days or more	280	12	▆
Don't know	1	-	
Total	2,357	100	

26 Mason V (1989) *Women's Experience of Maternity Care: A Survey Manual.* London, HMSO.
27 Department of Health (1997) *NHS Maternity Statistics, England: 1989-90 to 1994-5.* Statistical Bulletin 1997/28. London, Department of Health.
28 Ibid.
29 Audit Commission (1997) *First Class Delivery,* London, pp52-3. National data show the same picture: Department of Health (1997) *NHS Maternity Statistics, England: 1989-90 to 1994-5.* Statistical Bulletin 1997/28. London, Department of Health.

Figure 7   Mothers staying 48 hours or less (%)

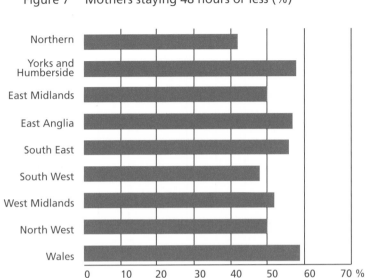

First-time mothers stayed longer after a normal or an instrumental birth, but around the same length of time as other mothers after a caesarean section. Type of delivery made a big difference to length of stay. Very few women went home early after a caesarean and, looked at another way, of the small number of women (280) staying for six days or more, 62% had had a caesarean (Figure 8, overleaf and Appendix Table 2.15). The duration of postnatal stay has been falling steadily since the 1970s.[30] This has implications for the quality of care in the postnatal wards (see Chapter 3) and means that more postnatal care is being provided by midwives in women's homes.

A number of babies needing extra care or observation were looked after with the mother in what is termed 'transitional care' - 186 women reported that this had happened. Two hundred and twenty mothers reported that their baby was admitted to a neonatal unit, and their care is described in Chapter 4.

30 Department of Health (1997) NHS Maternity Statistics, England: 1989-90 to 1994-5. Statistical Bulletin 1997/28. London, Department of Health.

Figure 8   Postnatal stay by type of delivery and for first time and other mothers

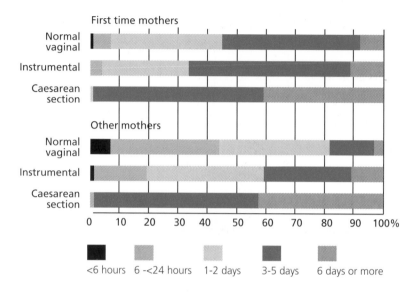

<6 hours   6 -<24 hours   1-2 days   3-5 days   6 days or more

Care at home after the birth

Midwives have a statutory obligation to provide postnatal care to the mother, whether at home or in hospital, for at least 10 days and up to 28 days after the birth. Daily visiting is no longer required, and policies vary between trusts. The various approaches to postnatal care have not been evaluated in terms of the benefits for women and babies.[31] All but 29 (1%) women had postnatal visits at home from a midwife. The babies of almost all these 29 mothers had been in the neonatal unit for more than 10 days (see Chapter 4). The pattern of visits up to the 10th day for the rest of the sample is shown in Figure 9 (and Appendix Table 2.16). In addition, 55% of women said that they had been visited by a midwife after the baby was 10 days old. A fifth of women were still being visited when the baby was over 15 days old, and 2% after the 28th day (see Figure 10 and Appendix Table 2.17). Women who had had a caesarean or instrumental delivery and women who had had twins or triplets, were more likely to be visited after the 10th day. Again there were regional differences in visiting patterns; women

31   Audit Commission (1997) *First Class Delivery*, London, pp56-7.

in the north and north-west of England were more likely to be visited beyond the 10th day than women in the south east and east Midlands (Appendix Table 2.18).

Because there is concern about conflicting advice in the postnatal period, women were asked about the numbers of midwives who visited at home

Figure 9   Visits at home by a midwife (up to the tenth day after the birth)

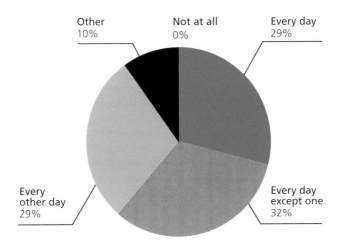

Figure 10 Age of baby at midwife's last visit

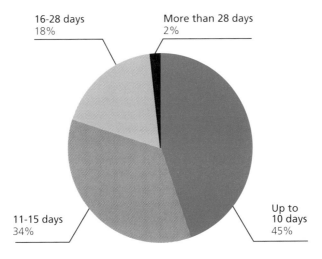

and whether they had met them before. Other studies have shown some variation between trusts in these aspects of care.[32] Only 16% of women were visited by one midwife at home, 44% saw two and 40% three or more in the course of the postnatal visits. A third of women had met all the midwives who visited after the birth, 48% had met some of them and 20% had met none of them.

Sixty-eight per cent of women reported that their GP had visited them to 'check on you and your baby's progress'. Women were asked if a health visitor had visited at home since the birth, and 99% said that one had. All but a small number of women (5%) had had their postnatal check by the time of the questionnaire. The check was carried out mainly by GPs (89%).

Women's health after the birth

Women were asked some questions about their health just after the birth (Table 13) and in the weeks that followed (Appendix Table 2.19).

Table 13   How did you feel physically during the first few days after the baby was born?

	No.	%	
Very well	541	23	
Quite well	647	28	
Tired and uncomfortable	763	32	
Exhausted all the time	242	10	
Very ill	157	7	
Total	2,350	100	

Table 13 is important in understanding women's needs for care and support in the period just after the birth. Seventeen per cent felt either very ill or exhausted, and a further third felt tired and uncomfortable. Women

32 Gready M, Newburn M, Dodds R, Gauge S (1995) *Birth Choices: Women's Expectations and Experiences.* London, National Childbirth Trust.

who had had a caesarean or instrumental birth were twice as likely to say that they felt very ill or exhausted (27%). After a home birth, nearly two thirds of the women concerned (32 out of 52) said that they felt very well, but they were a very small group who had had normal deliveries.

Women were also asked to think back and indicate whether they had had any health problems at ten days, one month and three months after the birth. The question was in the form of a list of problems which women could tick, and the responses are in Table 2.19 in the Appendix. The figures show that fewer than one in five women reported that they had had no health problems at ten days, and even at three months a majority of the women who answered the question were reporting problems. For most problems, the proportion reporting them declines over time. Depression is the exception to this, and backache also remains fairly common at three months. Other studies of postnatal morbidity show broadly similar overall levels of ill health, though the details of the symptoms, and the timing of the questionnaires are different.[33] The percentage of women reporting depression - 10% at three months - is within the range reported in most studies.[34]

Breastfeeding

Breastfeeding was asked about at several places in the questionnaire. Women were asked how, before the birth, they had planned to feed the baby, and 29% said that bottle feeding had been their intention. The rest had planned to either breastfeed or give mixed feeds. This proportion is very similar to that in the 1995 *Infant Feeding* survey,[35] though the question was asked in a different way. Seventy-two per cent of women reported that they had put the baby to the breast, if only once. The figure from the *Infant Feeding* survey is 68%. In hospital, 33% of women reported that their baby had only bottle milk, 48% had only breast milk, and 19% had both. The *Infant Feeding* surveys have shown that the proportion of breastfed babies given formula milk in hospital has declined over the last 10

33 Eg, Glazener C et al (1995) 'Postnatal maternal morbidity: extent, causes, prevention and treatment', *British Journal of Obstetrics and Gynaecology*. Vol. 102, pp282-7.
34 Eg, Brown S, Lumley J, Small R, Astbury J (1995) *Missing Voices: The Experience of Motherhood*. Oxford, Oxford University Press.
35 Foster K, Lader D, Cheesbrough S (1997) *Infant Feeding 1995*. London, the Stationery Office.

years, and that this is likely to be important because babies given formula milk in hospital are much less likely to be breastfed beyond the first few weeks.

By the time they filled in the questionnaire between three and four months after the birth, 30% of women were still breastfeeding and 38% had breastfed but stopped. Appendix Table 2.19 shows the proportions of women who reported breastfeeding problems when asked about the range of postnatal health problems they had had at ten days, one month and three months. Women who had given up breastfeeding by the time they completed the questionnaire were more likely to report feeding problems at ten days and at one month.

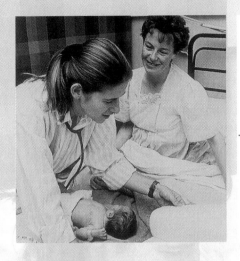

Chapter 3

Women's evaluation of their care

'I can't tell you strongly enough how much the midwifery unit improved my first few days with my baby. The breastfeeding was supported so well that we have not ever had any problems, and still enjoying. I had lots of support from the obstetricians down to midwife with my worries and fears when initially pregnant - miscarriage always at the top of any worries.'

'When I came up to the postnatal ward I felt very much like I was just left on my own to get on with things. This is wrong! We need help with this new and strange bundle!'

This chapter uses replies to the structured questions from the survey and written comments that women made in answer to an open question at the end of the questionnaire. It explores some topics that have either emerged from previous research or that are the focus of current policy, namely kindness, support and respect; confidence in staff; information and communication; options and choices for care; involving women in decision making; and women's views about continuity of carer, staff numbers and morale.[36]

Kindness, support and respect

Women were asked about the relationships they had with their care givers and whether they felt they were treated with respect. Similar questions were used for each phase of care. Overall ratings show similar results for care during pregnancy and for labour and delivery (Table 14). Between 50% and 60% of women *strongly agreed* that they were 'treated well as a person', that staff were 'kind and understanding' and that they were 'treated with respect most of the time'. Most of the remainder selected *tend to agree*. Depending on how you look at them, these results are either encouraging, because the majority of women agreed that care was good, or worrying because only just over half the respondents were able to agree strongly with the statements. Other studies have shown that maternity units differ in the ways that women rate their care, and that these differences are likely to be linked to the type of care provided, at least in part.[37] This means that care can be improved in this respect, and the final section of this report makes some recommendations based on this and other relevant studies.

For postnatal care (Table 15) women were asked about *all* care after the birth, covering both hospital and community based care. Just over half the women reported that, postnatally, staff treated them with respect *all the time*, and that they were kind and understanding *all the time*. These answers and those in Table 14 show the scope for improvement in the quality of care.

36 Audit Commission (1997) *First Class Delivery*, London, pp9-16.
37 Gready M, Newburn M, Dodds R, Gauge S (1995) *Birth Choices: Women's Expectations and Experiences.* London, National Childbirth Trust.

Table 14   How women assessed their personal care in pregnancy and at the birth

How strongly do you agree or disagree with the following statements?	strongly agree	tend to agree	neither agree nor disagree	tend to disagree or strongly disagree
	%	%	%	%
About the time during your pregnancy:				
I was treated well as a person (N=2,389)	51	38	8	3
The staff treated me with respect most of the time (N= 2,384)	51	37	9	4
The staff were kind and understanding most of the time (N=2,385)	54	36	8	3
About the time during the birth of your baby:				
I was treated well as a person (N= 2,342)	57	34	5	4
The staff treated me with respect most of the time (N=2,325)	56	33	7	4
The staff were kind and understanding most of the time (N= 2,331)	59	31	6	3

Table 15   How women assessed their personal care after the birth of their child

Thinking back to your care after the birth of your child, do you feel the staff who looked after you:	all the time	most of the time	some of the time	hardly ever or not at all
	%	%	%	%
Treated you with respect? (N= 2,386)	54	36	7	2
Were kind and understanding? (N=2,384)	51	40	8	2

Women were invited to write comments at the end of the questionnaire and these were classified by the researchers (see Appendix 1 for more details of this process). The desire to have supportive health professionals caring for them and understanding their needs was identified by nearly a fifth of the women making additional comments. These responses were fairly equally distributed, with 51% being classified as negative and 49% as positive. More than a quarter of women who indicated that they had felt well supported (28%) felt this about all aspects of their maternity care. Others emphasised support in the antenatal period (26%), during labour and delivery (18%) and at home after the birth (20%). A much smaller proportion made this type of comment about their hospital postnatal care (5%).

Fifteen per cent of those who added comments mentioned the attitude of care-givers; their comments were nearly always critical. They mentioned all stages of care (antenatal 33%, labour 23%, postnatal care in hospital 28%) but did not comment much on postnatal community care (8%). More of the comments about staff attitudes are about midwives (60%) than about hospital doctors (22%) and GPs (13%); this may in part be explained by the large number of contacts that women have with midwives over the whole of their care.

Some of the comments about care that was particularly good from a personal point of view are illuminating. For example the first comment below links 'respect' with more individual care. The second is about care that is very supportive and gives confidence.

> I'd just like to say that I think that antenatal care has improved so much since the birth of my first child six and a half years ago. You actually get treated with a lot more respect and you feel that the doctors/midwives actually care about your feelings and that you don't feel like you're just another pregnancy in a long line.

> The care received from my midwife was excellent. She was always there when I needed her, both before and after the birth. Nothing was too much trouble for her and she instilled great confidence.

Another facet of good personal care is shown in the next comment:

All the midwives and nurses that delivered all my babies made me feel very clever and made me feel like the only woman who had ever had a baby. All my experiences have been brilliant.

The small proportion of women who chose the most negative replies in the structured questions shown in Tables 14 and 15 clearly felt strongly and were more likely to write comments at the end of the questionnaire. For example, women were asked to agree or disagree with a series of statements about their care in labour. One was 'staff treated me with respect most of the time' and altogether only 86 women (3.7%) disagreed or strongly disagreed with this. In a similar way the statement 'staff were kind and understanding most of the time' was generally agreed with by the respondents, but 79 women (3.4%), often the same ones, disagreed or strongly disagreed. Some of their comments are helpful in understanding what had gone wrong. This woman was having her first baby:

My waters broke and I had to go in straight away. When you're worried and don't know what to expect, you need a kind smiling face to look after you and to say everything's going to be OK. In my experience I was met by a midwife who was very cold and who gave internals (vaginal examinations) when having very strong contractions. I was very unhappy about the way I was treated !

Two women made comments about disappointment when their wishes for care were not followed, and a third, who had not chosen a negative option in the questionnaire, described a better outcome to a change of plans:

I think (name of hospital) midwives should read personal notes before or during labour as I was very particular on certain aspects of my labour and these were ignored. I felt very annoyed afterwards and this has stayed with me.

The midwives ... didn't explain anything, tried to put me off my chosen pain relief because they didn't want to stay in the room all the time.

As I could no longer have my home delivery due to being induced, my daughter (aged nine) was very disappointed that she could no longer be present at the birth. With a little persistence the midwife who delivered me agreed to her presence and included her entirely. What a lovely experience.

One other woman who was very unhappy about her labour care indicated that she had been given an episiotomy against her wishes.

The other types of experiences described by women who had chosen the most negative descriptions of their personal care included having had pain that staff appeared to ignore, wanting help in the postnatal ward and not getting it, and feeling that staff disapproved of them or looked down on them. One young woman, aged 18 at the time she filled in the questionnaire, made a comment about the perceived attitudes of staff:

I did not like the midwives' attitude towards me after the birth of my baby, they thought that because I was young I was also stupid. They spoke to everyone around me as if I wasn't in the room. I asked for a different midwife to take over my care. I also had the same problem with my GP. He never seemed to believe me when I had medical problems during my pregnancy, also due to my age!

Some women commented on the way that women who had already had a child were assumed to need less attention or support.

Because this was my second baby and things were progressing well, I felt like I was 'just a matter of routine'. The fact that I felt low both physically and mentally was ignored.

After your first baby doctors and midwives don't seem to care as much. You often feel as though you just have to get on with it - not so many antenatal appointments and less sympathy if you feel you have any problems.

I feel more attention is paid to first-time mothers than second or third-time mothers. I was made to feel less important on my third baby, as if it was straightforward and I had less to worry about.

Although it seemed that some women's views of care as a whole were coloured by one bad experience, many others contrasted unsupportive care with all the rest of the care they had had. For example:

I found a great deal of support from my GP/midwife. I did not

*get the support on the postnatal ward (after I had the baby) I
thought I would. Saying that, I found one student midwife very
helpful but unfortunately not the others. I felt they did not have
time for me personally.*

*Did not 'get on' with the community midwife - she was very
'pushy' and critical - made me nervous of asking questions.
Health visitor was excellent - helped me through postnatal
depression.*

While personality difficulties between women and their carers will always
happen, some comments highlighted aspects of care, like privacy, which
can be audited and improved locally:

*While I had my legs in stirrups awaiting stitching, the staff in
the hospital, even those who had nothing to do with my
delivery, wandered in and out of the room. There was no
respect for my dignity.*

*I was in reasonably heavy labour during visiting hours and all I
had for privacy was a curtain around my bed, as there weren't
enough beds in delivery for me to be transferred.*

Confidence in staff

The questionnaire asked about women's confidence in staff in relation to
labour and postnatal care (see Table 16), and it also emerged as a theme
from their comments. Women were less confident in the staff that provided
their hospital postnatal care than at other times.

Table 16   Confidence in staff - labour and delivery care; postnatal stay in
hospital; midwives that visited at home after the birth

	always	sometimes	rarely and never
	%	%	%
Labour and birth (N=2,361)	77	21	2
Postnatal stay in hospital (N=2,341)	59	34	7
Midwives that visited at home after the birth (N=2,366)	75	23	1

Women were also asked about their satisfaction with hospital postnatal care, and only 46% said that they were very satisfied.[38] The relatively poor perception of postnatal care in hospital has been found in other studies. For example, in the evaluation of One-to-one midwifery care in west London,[39] women were much more likely to say that they were very satisfied with care at home after the birth than with postnatal care in hospital. There is also some evidence that this aspect of care may have deteriorated in the last ten years; in the four local surveys carried out in 1987 to test the OPCS Survey Manual questionnaire,[40] the proportion of women who were very satisfied with hospital postnatal care ranged from 76% to 83%. This is probably due to changes in the quality of care, but women may have higher expectations now, and the question was not asked in an identical way in the two surveys. Staffing problems in postnatal care are often mentioned by mothers and also by midwives in studies of care.[41]

Women who ticked the most negative options in the questionnaire were a very small proportion of the total, but were more likely to add their comments. For example 37 women (2%) answered 'never' to the question: 'Generally, during your postnatal stay in hospital did you feel confidence in those who looked after you?' Twenty-five of them, over two thirds, wrote a comment at the end of the questionnaire. Some were unhappy because of poor staffing, difficulty getting attention for their baby or lack of basic care like clean sheets. Some felt a lack of confidence in the skills of staff and their comments explain what had happened to them:

> *Appalling postnatal hospital treatment at (name of hospital) which contributed to depression re circumstances and method of birth. Four-month postnatal hospital treatment for infection contracted during caesarean in hospital.*

> *... but I must say that the doctors and midwives keep a lot of information and mistakes to themselves. Just like the placenta left inside my womb which caused me a lot of health problems and upset with my other children.*

38   Audit Commission (1997) *First Class Delivery*, London, p13.
39   McCourt C, Page L (eds) (1996) *Report on the Evaluation of One-to-one Midwifery*. London, Thames Valley University and the Hammersmith Hospital NHS Trust.
40   Mason V (1989) *Women's Experience of Maternity Care: A Survey Manual*. London, HMSO.
41   Eg, Garcia J (1997) *Changing Midwifery Care: The Scope for Evaluation*. Oxford, National Perinatal Epidemiology Unit.

Confidence in clinical care

More than half the women who wrote comments at the end of the questionnaire mentioned the clinical care or clinical skills of the staff who looked after them. Midwives were more likely to be mentioned in these comments whether they were positive or negative. Sixty-two per cent of the comments were classified as positive. Some examples include:

> I had bleeding at six months due to a low-lying placenta. I had to stay in hospital for a week. They looked after me really, really, well. They monitored the baby's heartbeat all the time. They were very thorough. I was very pleased with the way they looked after me and my unborn baby.

> My baby has a serious heart disorder (diagnosed at 11 days old) but the help I have received from my GP, health visitor and hospital staff has been very good.

> As a 40 year old insulin dependent diabetic I was surprised to find how enjoyable my pregnancy was made by the care and understanding shown by my GP and the AAU (antenatal assessment unit) and hospital staff.

Nearly half these positive comments (46%) were fairly general and did not refer to specific aspects of care, but there were very few of these positive comments specifically about postnatal care. Comments that were critical of clinical care and skill were more often made about labour care (37%) or postnatal care in hospital (26%). Some care was seen by women as clinically inadequate:

> I was tested for iron in January when I was three and a half months at my first hospital appointment and not again until May when it was discovered I was very low in iron. During that time I felt very ill and tired and had to finish work early. I wish I'd had regular blood checks, and that my doctor and midwife had listened and been sympathetic when I told them how ill I felt.

> I developed a severe wound infection following an episiotomy. This happened five to six days after the birth. I was at home and being visited by three different midwives, but they did not

> *realise until it was very severe. I lost all the stitches and had to be re-sutured three months later.*
>
> *The GP lost two of my blood test results, failed to test for anaemia ... and also failed to book me in ...*

One other theme that was repeated by quite a few of those who wrote comments was a wish that staff would give attention to women's experience from a previous birth, or give more weight to women's views of what they needed clinically. For example:

> *... to cut a long story short, I just wish they had listened to me rather than the monitor or the theory that the induction takes five and a half hours for the normal woman to work. If they had listened to me it would have made my pregnancy and childbirth a perfect one for me because even to this day - my child is five months old - when I think back to that day it makes me shiver and really angry ... They should listen to the main person who is giving birth, because only they know how it feels.*
>
> *As my previous baby to this one died of a strep infection passed on by me I was often concerned during this pregnancy and felt I was not given enough information about what could be done to stop it happening again as I am a carrier.*
>
> *My midwife insisted that I had a long way to go and that I should put off having pethidine for now as it would slow down the labour. I ended up being given my pethidine half an hour before the birth so it hardly helped me. If only the midwives would listen to us mums, especially when we've done it before.*

Comments of this type can be quite difficult for care-givers to accept because of their greater knowledge and experience, but it is likely that better communication and the chance to discuss the events may lessen women's feelings of not having been taken seriously. These issues are covered in the next section.

Information and communication

I found the whole experience very enjoyable. The care and support I received could not have been better. Every professional I came into contact with made me feel important, and listened to (and answered) many questions. Every stage of pregnancy and postnatal care was thoroughly explained.

Research about women's priorities for their care suggests that good information and communication are among the most important aspects of maternity care. For example, in a study carried out in maternity hospital,[42] women who had had a baby in the last few days were asked to score 40 aspects of maternity care on a scale from essential to irrelevant. Midwives and obstetricians also used the scale to record their assessment of what was important to women. At the top of the list women put 'the baby being healthy', and two items about communication: 'the doctors talking to you in a way you can understand', and 'having all your questions answered by staff'. In the MORI survey that was carried out for the Expert Maternity Group in preparation for *Changing Childbirth*,[43] women were asked: 'If you went through a pregnancy and birth again, what would matter most to you in terms of the care you were given?' The question was an open one - there were no preset categories for women to choose from. When the replies were coded, the biggest category, mentioned by 19% of respondents, was to do with continuity of carer, and the next was more information or explanation, mentioned by 13%.

In the present survey, women were asked whether there had been any help or support they needed in pregnancy and around the time of birth, but had not received. They were offered several categories and a free space for other needs (Table 2.20 in Appendix). Most women indicated that they had had all the support they needed (62%). Of the other options available, 'fewer different staff' was chosen by 18% of women, 'more information from doctors' by 12% and 'more information from midwives' by 10%.

42 Drew N C, Salmon P, Webb L (1989) 'Mothers', midwives' and obstetricians' views on the features of obstetric care which influence satisfaction with childbirth.' *British Journal of Obstetrics and Gynaecology*, Vol. 96, pp1084-8.

43 Rudat K, Roberts C, Chowdhury R (1993) *Maternity Services: A Comparative Survey of Afro-Caribbean, Asian and White Women Commissioned by the Expert Maternity Group*. London, MORI Health Research.

In the free comments at the end of the questionnaire, 20% of the women who commented (199 out of 983) mentioned information-giving or aspects of communication with staff. The majority of the comments were critical, and were more likely to refer to care in the antenatal period, where women have many contacts with staff and may have more need for information. Medical and midwifery staff were mentioned equally. Some of the comments highlight important aspects of this topic for women and these are mainly dealt with in the sections that follow.

Information in antenatal care

Women were asked whether they had known where to go for advice if they were at all worried during their pregnancy. Only 67 women (3%) answered 'no' to this question. These women were more likely to be from non-English-speaking backgrounds (one in five did not have English as a first language). The questionnaire went on to ask which professional a woman would have contacted first if she were worried or concerned. The GP and 'a particular midwife' were the point of contact for 28% and 36% of women respectively, and a further 21% of women said that they would contact 'any midwife'. Women who mentioned 'a particular midwife' seem to have also had better continuity in their postnatal care; they were far less likely to have known none of the midwives who visited them at home after the birth (9% v. 26%). On the other hand, they did not know more of the staff who cared for them in labour.

Part of information giving and communication is listening to women so that information can be provided that is relevant to their needs. Women were asked if they felt listened to, encouraged to ask questions, and whether staff talked in a way that could be understood. Table 17 shows the answers to these questions related to antenatal care in different locations. Only women who reported that they had had care in both locations are included in this table, but as can be seen from the numbers, this is a majority of women in the study (80%).

There were substantial differences in women's experiences of care in the different locations. In particular, women were far more likely to know the staff at GP visits.[44] Similar differences between hospital-based care and community care were found using a slightly different question in the test surveys for the OPCS Manual[45] and, more recently, in the Choices project carried out in Essex.[46] It is possible that women who have more complicated pregnancies may have a different experience of antenatal care in hospital. In the Audit Commission survey, women who said they had previous obstetric problems and those who reported five or more scans in this pregnancy were more likely to give positive answers to all four questions in Table 17. For example, just over half the women who reported five or more scans gave a positive answer to the question about staff in hospital who 'got to know you and remembered you and your progress from one visit to the next'. Table 17, therefore, is not a measure of the quality of care in a straightforward way. The findings could be seen as justification for encouraging community based care over hospital based care where clinically appropriate.

Table 17   For women who had some antenatal checks in hospital and some in the community (n=1,877) 'When you had check-ups at any of the following places, was there someone there (either a doctor or a midwife) who ...'

	Yes, at hospital clinic %	Yes, at GP surgery %
Encouraged you to ask all the questions you wanted to ask?	62	80
Would listen if you wanted to talk about your pregnancy and how you were feeling?	50	84
You felt gave you confidence?	40	80
Got to know you and remembered you and your progress from one visit to the next?	28	85

44 Audit Commission (1997) *First Class Delivery*, London, p12.
45 Mason V (1989) *Women's Experience of Maternity Care: A Survey Manual*. London, HMSO.
46 Gready M, Newburn M, Dodds R, Gauge S (1995) *Birth Choices: Women's Expectations and Experiences*. London, National Childbirth Trust.

In another set of questions women were asked whether they agreed or disagreed with a series of statements about antenatal care. Answers to two of these that concern communication are shown in Table 18.

Table 18   How strongly do you agree or disagree with the following statements about the time during your pregnancy:

	strongly agree	tend to agree	neither agree nor disagree	tend to disagree or strongly disagree
	%	%	%	%
Doctors talked to me in a way I could understand (N=2,369)	47	36	10	6
Midwives talked to me in a way I could understand (N=2,380)	66	29	3	1

Although this table shows that women found it easier to understand the information that they were given by midwives, it also indicates that midwives and doctors could improve this aspect of care. In answer to another question, it was found, as suggested above, that women with more complicated pregnancies were more satisfied with care from doctors than women with less complicated pregnancies. The findings shown in Table 18 are matched by similar results from other studies of maternity care,[47] but there has not been much recent research which has looked in more depth at what information women need and what they find difficult to understand. If care is to be improved in this respect we need to understand women's needs better.

Some of the comments made by women are helpful in understanding how communication can go well or badly. These two women were very happy with their communication with staff:

> *The midwife I had was absolutely brilliant. She answered all questions asked by myself and my husband and if she didn't know or was not sure, she would find out in time for my next visit.*

47 Eg, Gready M, Newburn M, Dodds R, Gauge S (1995) *Birth Choices: Women's Expectations and Experiences.* London, National Childbirth Trust.

The care I had while pregnant was excellent, especially from my GP who made time to sit and talk to me about what was happening and about any problems or anything I wanted to know.

Some women, though, had wanted clearer advice:

I would have appreciated very concise and clear advice on the 'do's' and don'ts' during pregnancy. I went to see my GP before I was pregnant for advice - he vaguely mentioned folic acid, but that was it. I found more advice in Sainsbury's on what to eat, etc.

Women's comments about antenatal care often refer to their need for good communication and tie this in with having smaller numbers of care givers, or ones they have got to know. This theme is picked up later in the chapter.

Information and antenatal screening

Clinical antenatal care is made up almost entirely of screening tests. Some, like regular weighing, urine testing or blood pressure measurement, are simple and seen as routine by staff and mothers. Others, like serum testing for Down's syndrome, are more technical, but may still involve only a blood sample from the mother. The results may have major implications for parents and can lead to a great deal of anxiety. This survey found difficulties in getting good information from women about some of the screening tests they had had in pregnancy. The questionnaire was filled in when babies were around four months old, and so some events in pregnancy may have been difficult to remember accurately. In addition, work in Manchester[48] has shown that women are sometimes confused about which screening tests they have had and for what reasons. Because of these uncertainties, the data about antenatal tests have to be treated rather cautiously. In this section we look at women's understanding of the tests, and satisfaction with the information provided to them.

48 Wray J, personal communication.

Table 19   Was the reason for having (screening tests) clearly explained
to you?

Test	Yes	No and don't know
	%	%
Ultrasound scan (N=2,382)	91	9
Blood tests (N=1,612)	91	9
Amniocentesis (N=109)	97	3
CVS (N=37)	95	5

Only small numbers of women felt that the tests had not been explained
(Table 19). Women who had higher levels of educational qualification were
less likely to say that the ultrasound scans had been explained; perhaps
their expectations were higher.

At the end of the section on antenatal tests, all women were asked if they
agreed or disagreed with the statement: 'Overall I was given enough
information about the risks and benefits of having different tests during
pregnancy.' Sixty-nine per cent agreed for spoken information, and 60%
for written information, leaving a substantial proportion who disagreed or
were unsure. Women's comments can give an idea of how important this
aspect of care is.

> *The consultant who did my CVS tests should get a medal. He
> was brilliant! Also the busy nurse involved made time to listen
> and that helped a great deal too.*

> *The medical staff did not have time to explain things like my
> amniocentesis test. The midwife advised that the doctor would
> explain the procedure, who in turn felt the midwife should have
> done this. I was given a leaflet, and it was left to the person
> operating the scan who was finally able to help me.*

> *I had a routine triple test and got a phone call to say that I had
> to go into the hospital the next day due to something being
> wrong with the baby. When we arrived at the hospital, we were
> kept waiting for 1½ hours and then saw the consultant. He was
> very uncaring and abrupt - told me I had a one in ten chance of
> my baby being Down's and shrugged his shoulders. We asked*

what happened now - offered amnio or accept it. There was nobody to talk to us about Down's - we were told to wait for the results of the amnio.

Some of the problems that women encountered with getting enough explanation about screening tests and dealing with the results need to be addressed in local policies and subjected to audit. In addition more in-depth research would help to find the best ways to provide information, and to deal with the needs of couples with problematic test results.

Communication during labour and birth

Forty-nine per cent of women said that the equipment and procedures in labour and delivery were explained *very well*, 37% *fairly well* and 12% *not very well* or *not at all well*. Women who described themselves as 'white' at the end of the questionnaire were more likely to give a positive answer to this question (87% v. 77%). Some of the women from non-English speaking backgrounds taking part in the survey may have had difficulty in understanding what was said, but, in addition, staff may have expected them not to understand and so may have limited their explanations.[49] Women were also asked to agree or disagree with two statements about understanding staff during the birth (Table 20). The results were very similar to those for the same questions about antenatal care shown in

Table 20   Please indicate how strongly you agree or disagree with the following statements about the time during the birth of your baby:

	strongly agree	tend to agree	neither agree nor disagree	tend to disagree or strongly disagree
	%	%	%	%
Doctors talked to me in a way I could understand (N=2,089)	42	35	15	8
Midwives talked to me in a way I could understand (N=2,336)	66	28	4	2

49 Bowler I (1993) 'Stereotypes of women of Asian descent in midwifery: some evidence.' *Midwifery*, Vol. 9, pp7-16.

Table 17 and suggest that this aspect of care could be substantially improved. Several studies that have used observation of labour care have shown how women's attempts to find out what is happening are sometimes ignored or diverted by staff and this is an area where research could now address ways of improving communication.[50]

Some women made comments about information and communication during labour and birth, though this was mentioned less often that it was for antenatal care. Two positive comments were:

> *The midwife I had during labour was really caring, explained everything he was doing. He never left anything out. He was fantastic.*

> *All the staff in theatre were excellent and talked to me and my husband through all the stages of the caesarean section operation. I felt totally safe.*

Lack of information or explanation can be very difficult for women and their partners:

> *I felt cheated. My husband and I had been through 30 hours of labour and neither of us were 'present' at the birth. I was not given the choice of being awake, and nobody explained why I had to have a general anaesthetic.*

It can also leave them with worries several months after the birth. For example:

> *I would have liked to discuss more why I was induced and was this the reason I had to have an emergency caesarean? I did ask the hospital doctor at my postnatal check, but he was pretty non-committal. I also asked him if any future pregnancies and births would go the same way and he said I would probably need another caesarean, but didn't explain why.*

50 Garcia J, Garforth S (1990) 'Parents and new-born babies in the labour ward' in Garcia J, Richards M, Kilpatrick R (eds) *The Politics of Maternity Care*. Oxford, Oxford University Press. Kirkham M (1989) 'Midwives and information-giving in labour' in Robinson S, Thomson A (eds) *Midwives, Research and Childbirth*, Vol. 1, London, Chapman and Hall.

Communication and postnatal care

In response to some of the concerns just mentioned, many trusts have begun to arrange for women to have the opportunity to discuss what happened at their delivery with someone who knew about their care.[51] This is felt to be helpful for some women, though research on the benefits and disadvantages has not been done. Women were asked if they had been able to talk to a staff member about the birth, while they were on the postnatal ward: 23% said that they did not want to, 23% that they had not been able to do this, 35% that they had been able to do this and a further 18% that they had sometimes been able to. One woman wrote:

> *I felt most of the time that the care I received was impersonal and rushed, especially in hospital after the birth of my daughter. I needed to discuss the birth and medical details, but was never given the chance or invited to.*

Some women wrote about longer term health problems that caused them concern. For example:

> *Since the birth of my child I have been left having to use a catheter tube occasionally to empty my bladder ... Myself, I have hoped it is temporary but at the same time feel fine in myself and glad my baby is born. Others blame my problem on the hospital and say I should seek further advice, or sue the hospital which I get annoyed about. A little advice would be lovely.*

One aspect of care provided in the postnatal period which can have important beneficial health consequences, is support for women who wish to breastfeed their babies.[52] The provision of consistent advice is important for this (Table 21).

---

51 eg, Charles J (1994) 'Birth afterthoughts: a postnatal listening service for women.' *British Journal of Midwifery*, Vol. 2, pp331-4. Smith J A, Mitchell S (1996) 'Debriefing after childbirth: a tool for effective risk management,' *British Journal of Midwifery*, Vol. 4, pp581-6.
52 Renfrew M J, Ross McGill H (1996) *Enabling Women to Breastfeed: Interventions Which Support or Inhibit Breastfeeding - A Structured Review of the Evidence*. Leeds, Midwifery Studies, University of Leeds.

Table 21   (a) If you breastfed your baby on the postnatal ward, did you feel you were given:

	Yes, always	Yes, generally	No	Didn't want this or don't know
	%	%	%	%
Consistent advice? (N=1,512)	31	39	24	6
Practical help? (N=1,499)	34	43	16	6
Active support and encouragement? (N=1,508)	39	38	18	4
Enough privacy to feed? (N=1,510)	49	39	10	2

(b) If you breastfed your baby at home, did you feel the midwives who visited you gave you:

	Yes, always	Yes, generally	No	Didn't want this or don't know
	%	%	%	%
Consistent advice? (N=838)	43	40	14	3
Practical help? (N=827)	41	41	13	5
Active support and encouragement? (N=836)	48	40	10	2

A quarter of breastfeeding women did not feel that they got consistent advice about feeding in the postnatal ward. Care in the community was somewhat better. This is an issue that is raised by women in many surveys. Privacy for feeding in the ward was rated as better than the other items in Table 21, but overall this question shows how much improvement could be made.

Choice

Two aspects of 'choice' were examined in this survey: the extent to which women felt that a variety of options for care were available; and the extent to which they themselves felt involved in the decisions that affected them (we have called this 'decision-making').

Options

The provision of as wide a range of options for care as possible is one of the aims of *Changing Childbirth*. However, many options are not widely available, and the decisions that women make about their care (or that are made on their behalf) can restrict options still further. Women were asked what options they had about the place of birth (Table 22). DOMINO births involve care from a community midwife in pregnancy and after, with the birth being conducted in hospital by the community midwife and medical staff if needed.

Table 22   Women's perceptions of the options available for place of birth **(N= 2,391)** (adds to more than 100% - women were able to tick more than one option)

What options did you have for where you would have your baby?

	Yes %
Going to one hospital in particular	65
The choice of different hospitals	31
GP unit at hospital	8
GP unit separate from the hospital	1
Having the baby at home	17
Having a DOMINO birth	13
I didn't know I had a choice	8

Forty-three per cent of the sample reported that their *only* option was one particular hospital; 77 women (3%) ticked only the last option: 'I did not know I had a choice.' Most of the other 124 women who ticked 'I did not know I had a choice' combined it with the first on the list 'one hospital in particular' and so were indicating that their choice had not extended beyond that. Some comments from women include:

> *I was told that I could only have my baby in hospital because it is the only option allowed by the midwifery service in the local health centre.*

> *I couldn't have the hospital of my choice as it was considered out of my 'catchment area'. I couldn't have the DOMINO birth which I really wanted due to 'lack of funds'. I didn't really have a lot of choice in where, who or how.*

It appears that only a minority of women (17%) thought that a home birth was an option and this is supported by the findings of the *Home Births* study,[53] which found that 25% of women in the hospital birth group had discussed a home birth, and that women in the home birth group were far more likely to have discussed their plans for the birth with care-givers and family. From the questions in the Audit Commission survey, though, it is not clear whether women were answering about the options they themselves had considered, or the options available to them in principle. In the *Choices* survey,[54] women were asked about options in a slightly different way (Were you offered the possibility of having your baby at home?). In that study, 13% of women said that they had been offered a home birth, and 6% a DOMINO.

Women were asked some other questions about options for care. Only 14% of mothers felt they had been offered a choice about which staff were present at the birth (a further 9% felt they had been partly and 74% felt they had had no choice). The choice of staff present was judged to be very important by 18% of women in this survey.

Involvement in decision making

> *With this pregnancy I felt I had so much more say in how things were done. I was made aware that in an emergency things would be done for the sake of my baby, and my preferences might not therefore be carried out ... Previous pregnancy was totally out of my control with a forceps delivery and a complete*

---

53 Chamberlain G, Wraight A, Crowley P (eds) (1996) *Home Births*. London, Parthenon.
54 Gready M, Newburn M, Dodds R, Gauge S (1995) *Birth Choices: Women's Expectations and Experiences*. London, National Childbirth Trust.

change of staff, none of whom I had seen before.

One way of looking at whether services are flexible and respond to women as individuals is to look at the extent to which women felt they had a say in whether certain procedures were undertaken, or how services were provided (summarised in Table 23). It is difficult to determine true 'choice', especially for some clinical issues, but the extent to which women feel involved in such decisions may be one indicator of the quality of the interaction with the professional, from the woman's perspective.

Table 23   Women's sense of 'having a say' in their care

Did you feel you had a say in / a choice about ....?	Yes %
Where antenatal check ups would take place	34
Who would carry out antenatal check ups	38
Whether to have a scan	52
Whether to have blood tests	73 (AFP)
	74 (Down's)
Whether to have amniocentesis	93
Whether to have CVS (*small sample)	84 (31/37)
Labour being induced	39
Labour being augmented	43
How the baby was monitored	20
Having an episiotomy	22
Whether to have stitches	13
Deciding when you went home postnatally	62

Some of the variation in women's answers to these questions makes sense when we look at the aspects of care covered. Where decisions have to be made quickly or where the woman might prefer to be guided by the professional, the low proportions reporting involvement in the decisions may be reasonable. For example, the decision about whether or not to stitch the perineum is probably one that most women would prefer to leave to the midwife or doctor, though a few may feel strongly. Some women

mentioned in their comments that decisions had had to be made in a hurry and that they were happy with this. To have a better idea about women's real involvement in decision making, including their own desire to be involved, it would be best to use other research approaches including interviews, or perhaps watching the care as it takes place.

Women were asked whether, before the baby was born, they had had any preferences about wanting or not wanting particular medical procedures or other things during labour. Over half of the women responding (57%) said that they did have preferences. Almost 80% of these women said that they had discussed their preferences with their midwife or doctor during pregnancy, and 62% said they were written down in their casenotes or in a birth plan. Women were more likely to comment about this if their plans did not work out as they wished:

> *Whilst in labour I had planned on having two people at the birth and this was not allowed, something I regret.*

> *I was planning for a water birth and was under the impression I would have one as long as there was no problems with the baby. I was just entering the pool when I was told it wasn't possible as my waters had been broken for more than 24 hours. I think this point should be made very clear beforehand, as it was a big disappointment to me and my husband.*

Of those women who had preferences, one in four said that their care did not follow their plan, mostly because their medical circumstances changed (two thirds of women gave this reason). A number of those whose care did not go according to their plans said that they had been advised to change their plans (21%), or that doctors or midwives did not take their preferences into account (5% and 11% respectively). Some of their comments have already been included.

One in three women (33%) said that they were not able to move around and choose the position that made them most comfortable for labour. There were many reasons for this, the most frequent being that the woman was attached to a drip or monitor (60%), she had an epidural (40%), or that the delivery was too quick (25%). Some women did not feel they wanted to move about (15%) and some felt that the staff did not encourage them to (15%). One in four (27%) women would have (definitely or possibly) liked to try an alternative position for giving birth.

Women were asked whether they felt their length of postnatal hospital stay was appropriate. Although 73% felt it was, the remainder were equally split between those saying their stay was too long or too short. Comments from women sometimes linked their short length of stay with staffing problems or with dissatisfaction about the quality of care on the postnatal ward.

In hospital, I wished to stay for two to three days but 12 hours after delivery I was told I may go home because they were so busy they wouldn't be able to give me the attention I needed.

I was very upset and disappointed with the postnatal care I received on the ward. At a time when I needed expert help and care with my baby's first few days, I never received it and I took the decision to leave hospital earlier than I had originally intended.

Sixty-two per cent of women felt that they had a say in the decision about when to go home, and those expressing this view were nearly twice as likely (83% v. 46%) to report that their length of stay was 'about right'. Similarly, for postnatal home visits by midwives, although 80% of women were satisfied with the frequency of visits, 13% felt they would have liked to see the midwife less often, and 7% more often.

Care-givers and continuity of carer

Unlike my first pregnancy and birth, during this pregnancy and birth I was fortunate enough to have the same midwife. I felt this made a great deal of difference, giving continuity and a real peace of mind and a dignity to the whole process.

Recent maternity policy has placed a great deal of emphasis on providing a personalised service. There is considerable debate about the best way of providing a personal, high quality service, within available resources.[55] Some trusts arrange for women to receive care from a limited number of different care givers, so that they have met antenatally the midwife or

---

55 Audit Commission (1997) *First Class Delivery*, London, p15.

doctor who looks after them in labour, and if possible, had the opportunity to develop relationships with their carers throughout their maternity care. Other maternity units attempt to minimise changes of staff during labour, so that that particular aspect of care is 'continuous'. Others argue that a 'traditional' means of deploying staff, which has the potential to provide greater continuity antenatally and postnatally (but not in labour and delivery), provides the best solution.

Altogether 8% of those who wrote comments (83/983) referred to continuity of care or carer. Just over a third of the comments were positive, for example:

> *Having one midwife for all antenatal care and during labour was the best care I can imagine.*

> *I have had three other babies, but it was only with my fourth that I had a team of midwives that cared for me throughout my pregnancy - at the clinic, hospital and home - and then delivered my baby. It was wonderful knowing them. It gave me a lot more confidence in my care and the baby's. It was by far the best pregnancy, labour and birth because of this care.*

Another woman was happy with her care in spite of lack of continuity:

> *Despite having met none of the midwives during my pregnancy, all of them, from the one who attended the birth, to the ones on the ward, to those who visited my home following the birth, were wonderful and extremely professional.*

Although there were no questions in the survey that dealt with continuity of carer in the antenatal period, it was the subject of comments from 23 women. These two women commented on the effects of seeing many different staff in the antenatal period:

> *Everybody I met was very helpful and friendly but it was very frustrating having to explain each time I went to a check-up who I was, etc, because it was always a different person and they would often make mistakes or misread my notes - which was very worrying, especially near my delivery.*

> *I had very frequent visits to the antenatal clinic at hospital because of a painful fibroid. During these visits I saw lots of*

different doctors, with different ideas, telling me sometimes contradictory advice and always having to read through my notes because they knew nothing about me. It made me feel that these visits were pointless unless I was lucky enough to see the consultant.

As illustrated in these examples, quite a few of the comments about continuity referred to the difficulties of having to explain things to different members of staff, and women's worries that clinical care might be less good when many care-givers were involved.

Women were asked about the importance of having the same staff throughout labour and about having met the staff before labour. Overall, having continuous care throughout labour was rated as more important, with 48% saying it was 'very important', compared with 24% who said it was very important to have met the staff before. However, different sub-groups of women hold different views on this. For example, those who had met the staff before labour were significantly more likely to rate this as important. This can be interpreted in a number of ways, but it may be that once this sort of care has been provided, it will raise expectations of the service, and will come to be in greater demand. There is also the possibility of disappointment if plans change.

Once I was in labour my first midwife and a student were very good and I felt very happy to have them. I later felt upset when their shift had finished and another midwife took over. It would have been better to have kept the first midwife all the way through as I felt I had a bond with her.

I was lucky to have had only one midwife with me in the delivery suite. This was very important to me. I did not have to experience them changing shifts. It made it a much more personal experience. Just me, my husband and the midwives (who I had not met before, but that didn't matter).

Some women were very happy with the continuity they experienced in labour. This mother compared it with a previous birth:

My first delivery was with a selection of different midwives and students who came and went as they pleased which I found very distressing and upsetting. My most recent delivery was totally different. So much different - it was wonderful to have a midwife I had met before and who stayed with me the whole time - I just wish this had been the case the first time as I am sure that it wouldn't have been so horrendous or distressing if this had been the case.

Support in labour is provided by professionals, of course, and also by women's birth companions. Two thirds of women (68%) said that they and their companions were left without professional support at some time during labour. One in four of these (24%) said that this happened at a time when it worried them to be alone. Nine tenths (93%) of women had a companion with them in labour, and all but 6% (124 women) of these reported that the companion was with them as much as they wished. Of the 124, 34/78 (44%) who answered the question said that this was because the staff would not allow them to be there as much as they would have liked.

Continuity of hospital postnatal care was not covered in a question, but was raised in some comments.

I was very pleased with the care I received before and after my baby was born - I saw two midwives mainly and came to think of them as friends. My stay in hospital was not quite as good because they were so busy and I was looked after by too many midwives on the postnatal ward. Every time I rang for assistance with feeding I saw someone different and had to explain my difficulties over and over again.

Poor continuity may lead to conflicting advice, and this can be very difficult for a mother to handle.

In hospital everyone kept giving me conflicting advice - eventually I learnt to ignore this, but as a new mother you take everything as gospel. This was a very confusing time. No one really sat and talked to me about how I was feeling and what were my fears and expectations

During my stay in hospital after having my baby I found the midwives contradicted themselves. One advises you to do one thing, the other sees you and tells you off like a naughty school child. I found this happened to most mothers on the ward, and I experienced it after having my first baby as well.

Long labour meant I was very tired. When I think back to my time in hospital, I remember craving sleep and being unable to get any due to staff interference. Totally inconsistent advice given whilst on ward. When you took one person's advice someone else would come in and condemn that practice. I severely fell out with one ward sister due to this ...

Changes in the organisation of midwifery, with more opportunities for women to be cared for by a small group of midwives through all phases of care, may lead to some specific problems in hospital postnatal care because of the unpredictable timing of women's needs for midwifery support when they are in the ward.

In postnatal home visiting, 40% of women reported receiving visits from three or more different midwives. The midwives were not always known to the women, with only one in three (32%) having met all of them before, and almost half having met some (48%). Women who had visits from more midwives were less likely to have met them before. In addition, women whose visits went on for more days after the birth were likely to be visited by more midwives. More than two thirds of women (71%) said that it mattered to them to have met the community midwives before. Women who had met all the midwives before reported more consistent advice, more active support and more practical help with breastfeeding. They were also more likely to think it mattered a great deal to have met the midwives before the birth. One woman had had a particularly bad experience of postnatal care at home:

I had six midwives visit at home afterwards and felt degraded, with so many strangers telling me to show them my stitches. I was treated like a number, and hated being called 'mother'.

Most women, though, reported that their home postnatal care was good; three quarters of women said that they were always confident in the midwives who visited at home after the birth (see Table 16 above).

Staffing

In addition to their concerns about continuity, many women mentioned staff shortages, particularly in relation to labour care and postnatal care (this was not asked about in the questionnaire). Out of 119 comments classified as being about the organisation of care, 55 were critical about staffing problems. Women were often sympathetic to the efforts that staff were making, but were very much aware of the pressure that they were under. They mentioned low morale among staff and staff comments about working arrangements. Some women tied their comments to their perception of the choice they had had about length of postnatal stay. These three comments are fairly representative:

> *Since having my first baby in 1991, I have noticed a decline in the resources available at the local hospital. There were noticeable staff shortages and the general impression was 'get them in and get them out as quickly as possible'. Women who have wisdom teeth out are given more time to recover!*

> *I felt that the midwife who delivered my baby was very rushed. I was left alone with my partner a lot. She seemed to have more patients than she could handle. Luckily it was my second baby so I had an idea of what was happening but if it was my first I think I would have been very frightened.*

> *Cutbacks have forced the closure of a ward, a reduction in staffing and a consequent loss of that vital teaching and reassurance that the midwives had so tirelessly and patiently provided. They felt helpless and frustrated - I felt let down. My heart goes out to all the young, first-time mothers leaving my local hospital now without the benefit of the teaching and expert advice I enjoyed five years ago.*

Several women made comments about financial pressures on the health service, including this one:

> *I feel the midwives who have looked after me and my baby have been very good and helpful. I feel concerned about the shortage of money which I have seen putting midwives and health visitors under a great deal of stress at times. Despite this I feel the service I have been given has been excellent and would be*

very sad if any further savings of money stretched resources so that things were not so good.

The other issue about staff that has come up in this study is occasional comments about tension or conflicts between staff. This was also raised in a recent study of midwifery group practices in the South Thames area.[56]

> *The care given in hospital for the birth of my first baby was excellent. However, the birth of this child was a dreadful experience. The general sense of malaise was appalling. Staff were offhand, argued with senior members of staff in front of patients, were unsympathetic, and generally the patients on the ward could not wait to leave.*

> *I was a DOMINO birth but on the night there was no DOMINO nurse on call so I was in the care of hospital staff who didn't know me and resented having to care for me.*

To be aware of tensions between staff is likely to undermine confidence at a time when women need to feel supported and be 'self-centred' rather than outward looking.

Good care

Identifying the elements of care that women found particularly good may be helpful at this point. Some of the most important things have already been referred to. Being treated as an individual is mentioned very often, and is linked to care that is not seen as routine. Not having to explain things to many different care givers can be a key part of individual care. Kindness and concern are obvious things to want at a stressful time, in a strange environment. Unfortunately, women's comments often refer to the absence of kindness - of being ignored, told off or criticised. Good care is also care that feels safe and competent, and that includes good communication. Here are some of the comments that women made about care that was particularly good. First a group of comments from women who had had problems in the past, or were particularly anxious:

> *As my waters broke at 25 weeks I was very distressed and frightened. Having to stay in hospital for seven weeks meant*

56   Allen I, Bourke Dowling S, Williams S (1997) *A Leading Role for Midwives*. London, Policy Studies Institute.

separation from my son and my partner. All the medical staff were sympathetic towards me and showed great support.

It took me some years to come to terms with losing my first little boy and to try again. In this pregnancy I was cared for very well and was admitted into hospital around the same time I lost my first baby. My consultant was a different one and was really great and came to talk to me nearly every day.

After many years of infertility problems and two miscarriages my pregnancy came as a surprise. The care and support we received was wonderful.

Then some comments to illustrate some of the dimensions of good care referred to above:

My midwife (name) is an excellent nurse who shows knowledge and compassion. She instils confidence in you and makes the birth easier - she's also kind and treats you as a person.

Just to say that the actual birth of my baby was wonderful. The staff at (hospital name) were great! They complied to all my wishes, were supportive and sensitive.

The midwife who delivered baby was wonderful. She talked me through the labour and gave my husband the opportunity to be actively involved. She was great.

Finally, quite a few women commented on ways that care had changed since earlier births. Here is one example from several where women felt that care had improved:

There are eleven years between my oldest and youngest children, and I am extremely happy about the increase in support, encouragement, empowerment and genuine respect over this time. I hope this will continue. Thank you.

Chapter 4

Women's experience of neonatal care

'After the birth we weren't sure if the baby was breathing. He was just rushed away by a doctor and we were not told anything other than not to worry.'

'I didn't like being in hospital on the same ward as all the other mothers who had their babies with them and mine was in special care.'

The issues for mothers whose newborn babies are admitted to neonatal care are complex. They and their babies may have health problems and are usually separated from each other at this time. Mothers in this position and their partners commonly find themselves isolated and anxious.[57]

Women whose babies require care of this kind are more likely to have had a history of problems, possibly with their own health, with previous pregnancy losses or with a previous baby admitted to a neonatal unit (NNU).[58] Their use of services through pregnancy, labour and postnatally is likely to be higher than mothers experiencing more conventional pregnancies and less anxious births. The need for more specialist care, for greater information and reassurance and a higher incidence of contacts with health professionals is likely to affect their experience and perception of maternity services.

Patterns of care postnatally are also likely to be different; in the immediate period following the birth, a mother and baby may be cared for in different hospitals. They may both be transferred from their local hospital, though not necessarily at the same time, for care at a specialist centre. The provision of hospital and community midwifery care for a mother whose baby has been admitted to a neonatal unit can be problematic. Transferring the baby to another unit or discharging a mother and baby separately can lead to difficulties in providing good postnatal care for the mother. The problems with unexpected admissions from home and transfers between hospitals are illustrated by some comments:

> *The shock of baby going into SCBU (special care baby unit) would have been lessened if he had been admitted from the ward and we hadn't been allowed to go home for one night.*

> *I was transferred to another hospital where my baby was treated extremely well in the neonatal unit. But I was treated like something the cat dragged in by the staff on the postnatal ward. This was a contrast to the hospital where my baby was delivered.*

57 McHaffie H (1990) 'Mothers of very low birthweight babies: how do they adjust', *Journal of Advanced Nursing*, Vol. 15, pp6-11; McHaffie, H (1996), 'Supporting families with a very low birthweight baby' in Robinson, S, and Thomson, A (eds) *Midwives, Research and Childbirth*, Vol. 4, London, Chapman and Hall; Redshaw M E, Harris A (1995) 'Maternal perceptions of neonatal care,' *Acta Paediatrica Scandinavica*, Vol. 84, pp593-8; Redshaw M E (1997) 'Mothers of babies requiring special care; attitudes and experiences', *Journal of Reproductive and Infant Psychology*, Vol. 15, pp109-20.
58 Redshaw M E, Harris A, Ingram J C (1996) *Delivering Neonatal Care: The Neonatal Unit as a Working Environment: A Survey of Neonatal Nursing.* London, HMSO.

Staffordshire University
School of Health
Royal Shrewsbury Hospital 'North'

Whose babies were cared for in neonatal units?

A total of 9% of mothers in the study had one or more babies admitted to neonatal care (220 out of 2,319), a figure that is comparable with national figures available[59] and with the data from the main Audit Commission study of maternity services.[60] They were equally likely to be women for whom this was a first pregnancy as women who had previously had a baby, but were likely to be younger on average (see Appendix Table 2.21, for these and other comparisons). Approximately one in five of these babies (22%) also went to the more intermediate facility of transitional care where the median length of stay was three days. Transitional care is care with the mother in a special ward, or part of a ward, where extra attention can be given to the baby. In some places, for example, phototherapy is given in a transitional care ward.

The most common reasons for admissions to a neonatal unit were prematurity and breathing difficulties. The study babies admitted to a neonatal unit had lower birthweights and gestations than those who were not cared for in this way (mean birthweight 2,700g compared with 3,400g; mean gestation 36 weeks compared to 40 weeks). A total of 31% were sick enough to need mechanical assistance with breathing (ventilation). Mothers who gave birth to more than one infant were more likely to have babies who were admitted to neonatal care (3% of the study population had multiple births and of these, 55% had babies who were admitted to neonatal care). The length of stay in neonatal care ranged from one to 100 days with an average of nearly two weeks (mean 13.3 days, median 7 days). Of the women with a baby in neonatal care, 40% had a baby who stayed for ten days or more. These data are similar to those from a recent large-scale study of neonatal care.[61]

59 Royal College of Physicians (1988) *Medical Care of the Newborn in England and Wales*. London, Royal College of Physicians.

60 Audit Commission (1997) *First Class Delivery*, London, pp58-9.

61 Redshaw M E, Harris A, Ingram J C (1996) *Delivering Neonatal Care: The Neonatal Unit As A Working Environment: A Survey of Neonatal Nursing*. London, HMSO.

Antenatal and labour care

Antenatally, these women were more likely to have CVS or amniocentesis, to have more of their antenatal checks in hospital than in the community and to have more ultrasound scans; a greater proportion had more than three overnight stays in hospital before the birth of the baby (see Appendix Table 2.21).

Mothers of babies in NNUs were significantly more likely to have experienced an operative delivery (58% compared with 27%) and more likely to have been delivered by caesarean than mothers whose babies were not cared for in an NNU (42% compared with 15%) (see Appendix Table 2.21). Of the caesarean deliveries, 52% were carried out as an emergency procedure, a proportion that is little different from that for mothers whose babies were not admitted to neonatal care (49%). However, the proportion of women who had their caesarean section under a general anaesthetic was significantly higher for this group (42% compared with 27%).

The women whose babies were admitted to neonatal units not only gave birth with more interventions, but were also more likely to describe the labour and birth as difficult. They were less likely to think that that the equipment and procedures used in labour and delivery were explained to them well at the time. This group had more medical involvement in the pregnancy and birth and, while pleased with this aspect of their care, they would have liked the care to have been more sympathetic and to have been given more information by the medical staff who cared for them. While the medical abilities and skills were valued by this group of women, who were aware of their own and their babies' need for specialist medical care, they also felt a need for better communication, especially in regard to the clinical decisions being made.

The perceptions of midwifery care differed little from the study mothers whose babies were not admitted to a neonatal unit, and nearly all of this group, like the rest of the sample, tended to agree that they were treated well as a person and with respect. Appropriately, it seems that greater care and attention were in fact paid to this group of women who were significantly less likely to be left alone in labour or shortly after the birth. The presence of a partner, not being left alone and feeling supported by both midwifery and medical staff at this time are likely to be especially important factors for women giving birth to a preterm infant or a baby with possible medical problems.

Postnatal care

The provision of effective and appropriate postnatal care may be a critical factor in assisting women recovering from more difficult births, coping with a sick baby in neonatal care and adjusting to not having the kind of experience they had wished for or anticipated.

Women whose babies were admitted to neonatal units were likely to stay longer in hospital than other mothers (see Appendix Table 2.21). A need for support and information was often expressed at this stage, with emphasis on the wish to understand what happened during the pregnancy and at the birth. These women were more likely to say that while in hospital it was very important to be able to talk to a member of staff that they knew, and indeed a higher proportion of the women in this group had been able to talk to staff about the birth of their baby. This was perhaps important in view of the fact that at ten days, one month and three months post-partum, significantly more of these mothers reported that they had suffered from depression (at three months the figures were 15% compared to 9%).

While some women with babies in neonatal care were able to talk to hospital staff, they may have missed out on some of the routine postnatal contact with midwives in the community. Their baby may have been in a hospital some distance away and, whether the unit was distant or not, they are likely to have visited the unit frequently and consequently not been at home much of the time. A total of 12% of women had babies who were cared for in more than one unit and, of these, a small proportion had babies who were admitted to three or more NNUs. In these circumstances continuity of care is difficult, if not impossible, and some women missed out on care and support at a time when it was most needed. Some units have liaison midwives or health visitors whose aim is to improve communication and care.

While the baby was still in hospital, relatively few of these women were seen by their community midwife (34%), GP (13%) or health visitor (16%). Obviously the duration of their own postnatal stay will have affected contact of this kind. Overall, women with a baby in neonatal care were more likely not to be visited at all by a community midwife at home (12% v. 1%), though all these had babies with long neonatal stays. By the time they filled in the questionnaire, they were no less likely to have been visited by a health visitor (99%) or a GP (59%) than other mothers. Postnatal care for women with a baby in a neonatal unit should probably be planned individually, with someone having clear responsibility for making sure that they do not get missed.

One woman wrote:

> *After I had my twins I stayed in hospital for two weeks as one of my babies was born with a cleft lip and palate and needed an operation. After I left hospital I was visited by no one, and I was a bit scared having twins and with my other children, but I managed. It would have been nice to see a midwife for a couple of days after returning home.*

Having a baby in neonatal care

The precipitate nature of their baby's admission to a neonatal unit is emphasised by the fact that nearly three-quarters of the women had babies who were admitted straight from the labour ward or operating theatre (73%) (Table 24). Mothers' anxiety and concern about the baby's well-being is not surprising in these circumstances.

Table 24   Timing and reasons for admission to a neonatal unit

When	Number	%	Why (more than one reason possible)	Number	%
Immediately after birth	160	73	Prematurity	109	50
From the postnatal ward	41	19	Breathing problems	69	32
From another hospital	4	2	Feeding difficulties	43	20
From transitional care	7	3	Observation	73	33
Other	7	3	Other	58	27

What does seem to be important for women is that they experience sensitive and appropriate care, especially in the early days after the birth, that they have contact with their baby and that they receive appropriate and accurate information about their baby's problems.[62]

62 Audit Commission (1997) *First Class Delivery*, London, p64.

After the birth of my baby, while we were both in hospital but separated, my needs and feelings were not taken into consideration or treated sympathetically by the staff on the postnatal ward.

The special care baby unit staff didn't always listen to our wishes with regard to our baby's feeding problem.

Most women felt that to a reasonable extent their baby's problems and the technical equipment used with their baby were adequately explained to them. However, a quarter (25%) said they were given little or no information about equipment or procedures and nearly one fifth (19%) that their baby's problems were not discussed with them. These problems were more often reported by mothers whose babies did not stay in for long, but still occurred for around one in seven of those with a baby staying for more than two days.

We needed more information about our baby, but in a way we could understand.

Involvement in care, and gradually taking over responsibility for this from the neonatal unit staff, emphasises a mother's role as a parent and marks out progress towards discharge home. Expressing breast milk and tube-feeding are both activities by which women can contribute directly to their baby's care. More than two-thirds of mothers (150) reported that their babies were tube fed in the NNU and more than half (61%, 91) of these actually fed their babies in this way. A total of 41% (89) expressed breast milk and nearly half the mothers breastfed or attempted to breastfeed their baby.

Mothers with babies in neonatal care were asked about a range of issues that relate to visiting the unit (Table 25). While most felt that to some extent they were able to be with their baby as long as they liked and felt included in their baby's care, this was not always the case. One in five were not able to stay with their baby during ward rounds and smaller numbers felt they could not have the visitors that they wanted.

The special care baby unit that looked after my twins was perfect, except my family that wanted to see them was put off because they could only stand outside the room and look through the window.

Some did not find the feed times sufficiently flexible or the feeding
arrangements adequately organised.

> *Facilities for breastfeeding in SCBU were not very satisfactory -*
> *only one breast pump for all mums and only tubing for one*
> *breast at a time. No privacy from doctors, nurses and midwives,*
> *other mothers, fathers and their relatives.*

Table 25   Issues associated with visiting the neonatal unit

When mothers visited their baby they:	always	usually	rarely or never
	%	%	%
Felt able to be with their baby as long as they wanted	79	18	2
Could stay with their baby during the doctors' ward round	60	14	20
Felt they could have the people to visit that they wanted	50	31	16
Found feed times flexible enough	58	27	11
Felt included in their baby's care	72	21	5

The facilities for parents differ between units and not all the women were
aware of what was available. While many units do not have a play area for
other children, most have a sitting room for parents, a place to make
drinks, accommodation for mothers needing to stay overnight and some
kind of information booklet. It is thus of concern that for a quarter or
more of women these common facilities were not apparently available
(Table 26). It may be that some babies were in NNUs for such a short time
that mothers did not need the facilities listed; however, in introducing each
mother to the unit, such features should normally be pointed out or
provided.

Table 26   Awareness and use of facilities by women whose babies were cared for in neonatal units

Facility	Available to mother %	Used by mother %
A booklet about the unit	65	46
A place to make hot and cold drinks	74	49
Sitting-room for parents	72	38
Playroom/area for children	35	15
Overnight accommodation for mothers	62	26
Overnight accommodation for both parents	36	14

The women whose babies were cared for in neonatal units were also asked about the practical issues of visiting their baby. Problems in visiting occurred for 17% of mothers, most commonly due to their own poor health and travel difficulties. Some referred to the actual cost of travel and difficulties with looking after their other children when visiting the new baby.

Neonatal care is an expensive part of the maternity services, particularly in terms of the specialist staffing and equipment needed. Yet much of what mothers and their partners say they need in this context is not costly - the need for information and support is paramount. In many ways their needs differ little from those of other mothers who have recently given birth and their responses in the survey echo those of the main study group. However, women in this situation are more vulnerable. They are likely to need both more physical care, and higher levels of support, for a longer period. At the same time most mothers in this situation recognise that the care of their baby is the main priority, make very few demands in terms of their own needs and are very grateful for the care their baby is given.

> *The care given to me and my baby could not be bettered. The SCBU was first class.*

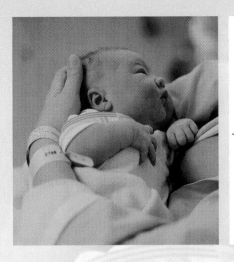

Chapter 5

Implications for practice and research

'My other two children are now young adults. Antenatal and postnatal care since their births has changed considerably and for the better. In my previous pregnancies I felt 'done-to' - having little explained, no choices and treated with little or no respect. My age and naiveté prevented me from asking questions and I therefore accepted my lot. Now I feel as if my child has been mine from conception. I've been encouraged quite rightly to take responsibility and decisions from the start and I have felt respected. I feel this is a good start to enabling parents to take responsibility for their children.'

Different readers will draw different messages from the results presented in this report. This chapter picks out some of the issues that the authors considered most useful or relevant. Maternity care is very important to women and many of those who filled in the questionnaire went to a lot of trouble to express their opinions. Women deserve to have their views taken into account, and local and national services should be planned in the light of studies such as this. Not all women want the same things; research can tap the variety of women's needs, but may need to use special approaches to reach those, like younger women or women from non-English-speaking backgrounds, who are less likely to complete questionnaires.

Although women's needs and wishes do vary a lot, there are some things that we can generalise about. Women want care that is technically good and well organised, where care givers communicate well and respect each other. Women appreciate the different skills brought to maternity care by the different professional groups involved. They need, and want, good communication with their care givers, enough information about what is happening and the opportunity to find out more if they need to. They want to be treated with kindness and respect, and when they are in pain or frightened they want support and help. They prefer to feel that they are individuals as far as the staff are concerned. Many women express gratitude towards the staff who look after them, and concern about the pressure under which they work.

The survey, and the local studies carried out for the main report, show a great deal of variation in the care that women get. A uniform approach is not the goal, since different places have different populations, and services will choose to give priority to different aspects of care. Equity, though, should be an important consideration when care is looked at nationally. Those who work in the service also deserve fair treatment; poor staff morale is bad in itself and may lead to worse care for women.

Implications for practice

Antenatal care

Many women are making a first contact with professionals very early in pregnancy and may then experience a 'gap' before formal antenatal care starts. Some commented on this and on their need for advice about their health and behaviour in the early part of pregnancy. Audit of early pregnancy contacts might be useful.

Many women did not feel they had any options about place of birth, place of antenatal care or care-givers for antenatal care. Information about local services is very important to allow women to take advantage of the choices that exist.

In this survey, the small sub-group of women having more of their antenatal care in hospital (14% of the sample) had a lower average number of visits, in spite of being more 'at risk'. Women may, perhaps, be more likely to arrange extra visits in community settings. Providing care in several locations may have advantages but may also tend to increase the total number of visits

In common with other studies over the last 20 years, this survey has shown that women were more satisfied with their communication with care-givers at local antenatal visits than in hospital, and that they were more likely to know their care-givers at local visits. These benefits need to be taken into account when planning care patterns.

Women were more likely to say that they understood what was said to them by midwives than doctors.

Care in labour

Some women commented on problems with isolation and lack of support during early labour in hospital. This is an area where audits of care and advice to women would be useful.

On currently available evidence, the use of the ventouse is recommended, where possible, for assisted vaginal births because it leads to less trauma for the mother. This survey has shown that forceps are still more commonly used, so further progress is necessary.

Some women reported that a reason for their planned caesarean section was having had a caesarean before. The Royal College of Obstetricians and Gynaecologists' recommendation on the basis of available evidence is that routine repeat caesarean should be avoided.

One woman in four would like to have tried a different position for delivery, though only a few felt strongly about this.

Episiotomy rates vary markedly between regions. There is no evidence so far that liberal use of episiotomy has benefits for women.

Twenty-two per cent of women who had stitches had to wait at least 20 minutes for the repair to be done.

Just under half the respondents were cared for at the birth by staff whom they had already met, and half were cared for by the same midwife throughout labour and birth. This and other studies have shown that women want better continuity of care in labour and birth, in both these senses. More women feel strongly about having the same midwife caring for them throughout labour if possible.

Knowing the care givers involved in labour and at the birth is very important for some women. Could this be provided selectively, for those who might benefit from it most, in places that do not aim to make it available to almost all women?

Postnatal care

Around a quarter of women would have liked to talk about their birth with a member of staff in the postnatal period.

Postnatal care in hospital is less satisfactory than other aspects of care. This survey and other recent studies give some indications of how care might be improved, but proposed changes should be evaluated.

Women perceive hospital postnatal care to be under-staffed by midwives.

There are differences between women's expectations of the help they will get for themselves and the baby in the postnatal ward and what they receive. Other studies have shown that this is particularly a problem for women from some minority ethnic groups, but the present survey found comments on this from women of all backgrounds.

Support for breastfeeding could be improved for a substantial minority of women, both in hospital and at home.

Forty per cent of women are visited by three or more midwives at home after the birth, and this is likely to reduce the quality of their care.

Postnatal health problems are common, with four-fifths of women reporting one or more problems at ten days. Some women commented on serious or long lasting problems for which they had found it hard to get help.

Postnatal care for women with a baby in a neonatal unit should probably be planned individually, with someone having clear responsibility for making sure that they do not get missed.

Some women with a baby in a neonatal unit do not get enough information about their baby and the care provided.

Implications for research

The very early part of pregnancy has not received much attention from researchers, partly because it has been difficult to find samples of women to study. There are cost implications of women seeing a GP or midwife very early, and there is a need to look at women's wishes for advice and information.

Women's needs for information about antenatal tests, and their experiences of getting the results of tests, are not well suited to retrospective postal questionnaire methods. A review of appropriate research in this area, including some important unpublished studies, would be helpful to planners and providers of services.

Regional variations in the pattern of antenatal care and the use of ultrasound should be explored further.

Patterns of antenatal care with different care-givers, in different locations, are poorly documented in routine sources, yet care is very diverse and this has cost implications. We know little so far about women's wishes about place of care and which care givers should be involved, but what is known from smaller studies suggest that many women want contact with all the main care-givers - midwives, GPs and obstetricians.

Local audits of antenatal home visits should be carried out and policies formulated. In addition researchers could address women's wishes for care at home, and the cost implications.

Knowing the care-givers involved in labour and birth is associated with some improved outcomes in terms of satisfaction with care. This association may not be causal, and research using appropriate designs is needed to look at the clinical and psychosocial impact of having known carers.

What is meant by choice and how important is it for women? How do choice and information interact?

How can the personal quality of care be improved? What impact do staffing, staff morale and staff training have on the way that women are treated? Are 'leaders' crucial? Does feedback of women's views to staff improve care?

Appendices

Appendix 1 Methods and populations

The questionnaire was sent to women when their babies were around four months old and it covered their care in pregnancy, at the birth and after. The questionnaire was broadly based on that designed by OPCS (Office of Population Censuses and Surveys) (Mason 1989) although many questions were changed to reflect the issues of particular interest in the study. The questionnaire was designed by the Audit Commission study team, its external advisers, and MORI's health research group who were contracted to pilot and subsequently administer the survey during November and December 1995.

The questionnaire was divided into eight sections. The main scope of each section is described in Table 1.1.

Table 1.1   Scope of the questionnaire

Section	Scope
A Dates and your baby	Date of birth
	Gestation
	Whether singleton or multiple birth
B Antenatal care	Different professional inputs to care
	Different locations for care
	Casenotes
	Tests and scans provided
	Hospital stays during pregnancy
	Information for all of the above
	Preferences and choice for all of the above
	Satisfaction for all of the above
C Labour and birth	Options for place to give birth
	Place of birth
	Transfers during labour
	Birth preferences and birth plans
	Length of labour
	Interventions (induction, augmentation, type of fetal heart monitoring, episiotomy, stitches)

Section	Scope
Labour and birth (continued)	Methods of pain relief
	Mode of delivery
	Staff involved in birth and maternal attitude to staff (including continuity of carer)
	Staff support in labour
	'Having a say' in decisions about interventions and decisions in labour
	Explanation and understanding of reasons for interventions in labour
	Women's perceptions of experience of labour
D Babies born at home	Planned or unplanned
	Reasons for home birth
	Staff support for home birth
	Information provided regarding home birth
	Transfers to hospital following delivery
	How women felt after the birth
E Care in hospital following birth	Length of hospital stay
	Availability of debriefing facility
	Planned and actual means of infant feeding
	Support for chosen method of infant feeding
	Women's perceptions of experience of postnatal care
	Women's involvement in decisions in postnatal care
	How women felt after the birth
F The care of your newborn baby (special medical care)	Where baby was cared for
	Length of stay in NNU
	Reasons for admission of baby
	Transfers
	Explanation of procedures and equipment
	Involvement of mothers in care
	Information about the unit
	Postnatal care of mothers of NNU babies

Section	Scope
G Care at home after the birth	Patterns of home visits by midwives
	Preferences about home visits
	GP and health visitor home visits
	Postnatal check ups
	Postnatal ill health
	Infant feeding
	Satisfaction with care provided
H You and your household	Age
	Parity
	Ethnic group
	Language
	Disability status
	Previous pregnancies - ill health in mother or baby

Sample

A random sample of 3,570 women who had had a baby during June and July 1995 was drawn by OPCS (now the Office for National Statistics) from birth registers of all registration districts of England and Wales. Of the 3,570 women sent a questionnaire, 2,406 women responded, giving a response rate of 67%. No reminders were sent, as the returned questionnaires were not identifiable.

How representative are those who replied?

It is possible to check if the sample drawn by the Office for National Statistics was reasonably representative of births in England and Wales for that year, and also make some comparisons between those who completed the questionnaire and those who did not. Survey respondents usually differ from the population from which they are drawn. In maternity surveys, for example, women who are younger and poorer are less likely to take part. Women from non-English-speaking backgrounds are also less likely to respond. The tables below compare selected characteristics of respondents with the survey sample and with data from Birth Registration, the General Household Survey and the Census.

Table 1.2 shows that the sample population was representative of the population having births in that year, but that younger women (under 25) were less likely to respond. Table 1.3 shows that women who were coded as 'economically inactive' were somewhat less likely to respond. There was no difference by region of residence (Table 1.4).

Table 1.2 Age of respondents

	Maternities in England and Wales in 1995* %	Total sample population %	Respondents %	No.
Age				
<20	7	6	4	(88)
20-24	20	20	16	(391)
25-29	34	34	33	(791)
30-34	28	28	33	(787)
35-39	10	10	12	(292)
40 or more	2	2	2	(57)
Total	100 (642,404)	100 (3,570)	100	(2,406)
Mean age			29 years	

* Source: ONS (1997) *Birth Statistics 1995*. Series FM1, No. 24, London, the Stationery Office.

Table 1.3 Occupational classification

Social Class (OPCS classification - women's occupation)	Total sample population N= 3,570 %	Respondents N= 2,359 %
Prof / intermediate	20	23
Skilled non manual	25	29
Skilled manual	5	6
Partly skilled	8	8
Unskilled	1	1
Economically inactive	40	34

Table 1.4   Regional distribution

Region	Births in England and Wales in 1995 N= 628,901 %	Total sample population N=3,570 %	Respondents N=2,356 %
North	6	5	5
Yorks & Humberside	10	10	10
East Midlands	7	8	8
East Anglia	4	4	5
South East	37	38	37
South West	8	9	10
West Midlands	11	10	10
North West	12	11	11
Wales	5	5	5

Table 1.5 suggests that women with no educational qualifications were under-represented among the respondents. Table 1.6 shows that women from minority ethnic groups did take part in the survey, though the numbers in each category are small. English was not the first language of 139 respondents (6%).

Table 1.5   Educational qualifications of respondents

Highest level of educational qualification (excluding professional qualifications)	Audit Commission survey (N=2,406) No.	%	General Household Survey 1993 (No.24) (Women aged 16-39) Great Britain No.	%
None	293	12	671	20
GCSE / CSE / O level	989	41	1,565	46
A level or higher	1,096	46	1,071	32
Not stated / Other	28	1	65	2
Total	2,406	100	3,372	100

Table 1.6   Self-assigned ethnic group of respondents

	Audit Commission Survey		1991 Census data women aged 15-44
	%	No.	%
White	91.9	2,210	93
Other ethnic groups combined	7.4	179	7
Consisting of :			
Black British	0.7	18	
Black Caribbean	0.6	14	
Black African	0.7	18	
Black other	0.1	3	
Indian	1.5	35	
Pakistani	1.3	32	
Bangladeshi	0.3	8	
Chinese	0.2	4	
Other	2.0	47	
Not stated	0.7	17	

Table 1.7 shows some aspects of women's maternity care. In general the survey figures compare well with those from national data. Relevant comparisons are discussed in more detail in Chapter 2.

Table 1.7   Summary description of study sample

	Study Sample		National data
	No.	%	%
Place of birth			
Hospital	2,308	96	98
GP unit at the hospital	33	1	
Home	52	2	2
Planned	(36)		
Unplanned	(16)		
Other	8	<1	1
Total	2,401	100	Source: Birth Registration*
Parity			
First baby	1,015	42	45
Subsequent baby	1,387	58	55
Total	2,402	100	Source: HES**
Labour			
Induction	626	26	20
Total	2,389	100	Source: HES**
Mode of delivery			
Caesarean section - planned	212	9	6
Caesarean section - other	204	9	9
Forceps	150	6	9
Ventouse	131	5	5
Normal vaginal	1,707	71	70
Total	2,404	100	Source: HES**
Episiotomy	547	23	20
Total	2,381	100	Source: HES**

*   ONS (1997) *Birth Statistics 1995*. Series FM1, No. 24, London, the Stationery Office.
**   Department of Health (1997) *NHS Maternity Statistics, England: 1989-90 to 1994-5*. Statistical Bulletin 1997/28. London, Department of Health.

Women's written comments

Many women (1,042, 43% of respondents) provided additional written comments in response to the question: 'Is there anything else you would like to tell us about your care while you were pregnant or since you have had your baby?' These women were somewhat different from the respondents as a whole. Women having their first baby were more likely to comment (50% compared to 38%), as were older women and women who had continued in full time education beyond GCSE or O-level. Women who described themselves as having had a difficult birth were more likely to comment (52% of those who had a difficult delivery - ventouse, forceps or caesarean section - compared with 40% of those who had a normal vaginal delivery). In general, women who ticked the most negative options in the questions about their care were more likely to comment, and they often used the opportunity to describe what had happened to them (see examples in Chapter 3). On the other hand, many women with good experiences added comments.

Some women's comments covered more than one issue and up to three of these issues were coded by a researcher. This led to 1,559 comments which were coded in four ways.

1 **Stage of care referred to:**
antenatal; labour and delivery; postnatal; neonatal and service as a whole

2 **Theme:**
thirteen themes were identified including communication, skill, choice, information

3 **Whether the comment was positive, negative or neutral**

4 **Whether specific staff categories were referred to**
such as GP, midwife, etc.

Overall, twice as many of the 1,559 comments were judged to be negative rather than positive; a few were neutral. Many women made both negative and positive remarks. The analysis of the themes covered in women's comments is used in Chapter 3.

The survey's potential

The figures in the Tables above show that although some social categories of women were slightly under-represented, the women who sent back these questionnaires were fairly typical in terms of geographical area of residence and types of care received. The sample size is large for a survey of women's views and so a wide range of experiences is represented here. It is very unlikely that women who did not respond to the questionnaire had such different experiences of care that, had they taken part, the main conclusions would be altered. Women put in a lot of time to fill in the questions and add comments, and it was clear that some were either writing in an unfamiliar language or found writing difficult.

There are some limitations to the method used. For example, because it is filled in about four months after the birth, some details of care in pregnancy may be difficult to remember. Women were asked to recall their feelings, and their memories may be affected by the good or bad experiences that they had since or because, for example, their baby had been very ill. A retrospective survey of this kind cannot disentangle these effects.

The study is most useful as a measure of women's experiences and feelings about care. It was not designed to answer questions about whether care is effective or appropriate. In spite of the large sample size, there are some topics that the study was not big enough to deal with. For example, only 52 women who had had a baby at home were part of the sample, and only one gave birth in a GP unit away from a large hospital. This means that their experiences cannot be compared with those of other women. A large study of home births has recently been published, however (Chamberlain et al, 1996).

Some other categories that are represented only by small numbers of replies are very young women, and women with disabilities. We would suggest, though, that an 'all purpose' survey is probably not the best way to look at experiences of particular categories of women. For example, the present questionnaire did not ask about some key issues for women with disabilities such as access to care, facilities and specific discussions with staff about medical conditions. It can, though, give figures against which such special studies can be compared.

In spite of these limitations, which are common to most large cross-sectional surveys, the study gives a much fuller and more representative national picture of maternity care than has been available for many years. In the report, comparisons are made with some recent local studies of women's views of care, and with national data from sources such as the five-yearly Infant Feeding surveys carried out by the Office for National Statistics, and recently published Hospital Episode data.

Analysis

The questionnaires were coded, and analysed using computer packages, and the women's written comments were transcribed. We have followed the policy of not drawing attention in the text to differences that are likely to have occurred by chance (in other words that are not statistically significant). Because of the study design, though, even statistically significant associations between variables within the dataset have to be interpreted with caution. For example, women who had an epidural were far more likely to have a long postnatal stay in hospital. This finding is misleading, however, as the association may not be causal. It results from the fact that first time mothers are more likely to have an epidural and also a long postnatal stay. When we look at first time mothers only, we find no link between length of stay and use of epidural analgesia.

Appendix 2 **Tables**

Table 2.1   Weeks of pregnancy at time of first discussion of maternity care

Time of first contact	No. of mothers	% mothers
0-6 weeks	904	38
7-11 weeks	1,027	44
12-20 weeks	398	17
Over 20 weeks	29	1
Total	2,358	100

Table 2.2   Number of antenatal visits

No. of visits	No. of mothers	%
1-5	127	6
6-10	609	26
11-15	1,028	44
16-20	404	17
21+	148	6
Total	2,316	100

Table 2.3   Regional distribution of antenatal visits (total number of visits)

Region	Low AN visits (1-10 visits) N=719		Medium AN visits (11-15 visits) N=1,004		High AN visits (16+ visits) N=546	
	No.	%	No.	%	No.	%
North	24	19	56	45	44	36
Yorks & Humberside	79	35	97	43	51	23
East Midlands	40	22	81	44	62	34
East Anglia	29	28	53	52	21	20
South East	338	41	336	41	150	18
South West	62	28	112	51	47	21
West Midlands	57	26	104	47	59	27
North West	64	26	107	43	76	31
Wales	26	22	58	48	36	30

Table 2.4 Regional distribution of antenatal visit pattern

Region	More hospital visits N=306 No.	%	More community visits N=1,859 No.	%	Equal nos hospital and community visits N=546 No.	%
North	12	10	104	84	8	7
Yorks & Humberside	25	11	191	84	10	4
E Midlands	19	10	157	86	7	4
E Anglia	12	12	86	84	5	5
S East	127	15	656	80	39	5
S West	18	8	195	88	8	4
W Midlands	25	11	191	87	4	2
N West	45	18	190	77	12	5
Wales	23	19	89	74	8	7

Table 2.5 Distribution by age of women having CVS or amniocentesis compared with the whole sample

		Age Group					
		15-19	20-24	25-29	30-34	35-39	40+
CVS or amniocentesis	No.	3	6	21	34	67	13
(N=144)	%	2	4	15	24	47	9
No CVS or	No.	72	348	725	718	211	42
amniocentesis	%	3	16	34	34	10	2
Whole study	No.	75	354	746	752	278	55
sample (N=2,260)	%	3	16	33	33	12	2

Table 2.6   Timing of first scan (gestational age in weeks)

No of weeks	No.	%
2-5	34	1
6-10	435	18
11-15	773	33
16-20	1,019	43
21-25	68	3
over 25	38	2
Total women	2,367	100

Table 2.7   Proportion of women having different numbers of scans and experiencing different kinds of care (%)

Of women having different numbers of scans	Low	Medium	High
No. of scans	(1-2)	(3-4)	(5 or more)
No. of women	1,325	734	324
Percentage of women	56	31	14
Previously given birth	59	53	64
Aged 15-24 years	20	20	21
25-34 years	68	64	61
35 and over	12	17	18
Adverse obstetric history	19	27	38
1-10 antenatal checks	35	30	23
11-15 antenatal checks	47	44	34
16 or more checks	19	26	42
Overnight antenatal stays in hospital (3 nights or more)	6	18	35
Induced (excluding those who did not go into labour)	23	31	49
Continuous monitoring in labour (excluding planned caesarean section)	51	54	64
Caesarean section delivery	13	17	36
Planned caesarean section	6	8	21
Operative vaginal delivery	11	13	13
Delivered their baby preterm	8	13	30
Had a baby who was admitted to NNU	6	12	22
Multiple birth	<1	1	19

Table 2.8   Which members of staff were *present* in the room when your baby was born? (Tick as many as applied)

Staff present	No. of women	%
Midwife	2,260	95
Student nurse or student midwife	599	25
My GP or family doctor	69	3
Obstetrician	784	33
Paediatrician	660	28
Anaesthetist	508	21
Trainee doctor	206	9
Nurse	500	21
Medical student	135	6
Ambulance paramedic	18	<1
Other	30	1
No professional staff	10	<1
Don't know/ under general anaesthetic	80	3
Missing	22	1
Total	2,406	

Table 2.9 Which members of staff were *actively involved* in delivering, and immediately caring for, your baby? (Tick as many as applied)

Staff actively involved	No. of women	%
Midwife	1,990	84
Student nurse or student midwife	355	15
My GP or family doctor	40	2
Obstetrician	598	25
Paediatrician	492	21
Anaesthetist	212	9
Trainee doctor	104	4
Nurse	316	13
Medical student	35	2
Ambulance paramedic	7	<1
Other	16	1
No professional staff	10	<1
Don't know/under general anaesthetic	80	3
Missing	22	1
Total	2,406	

Table 2.10 Some of the factors that may be associated with different types of delivery

Type of delivery		Normal	Forceps or ventouse	Caesarean section
		N=1,707	N=281	N=416
		%	%	%
Parity:	primips	36.3	72.6	46.3
	multips	63.7	27.4	53.7
Age:	15-24	21.4	18.9	14.4
	25-34	64.8	70.8	65.1
	35-40+	13.8	10.4	20.4
Adverse obstetric history		23.7	19.2	28.8
Antenatal checks:				
	1-10	31.6	29.8	33.5
	11-15	45.5	44.1	40.3
	16 or more	22.9	26.1	26.3
Antenatal scans:				
	1-2	59.7	50.5	42.4
	3-4	30.5	34.4	29.5
	5 or more	9.8	15.1	28.1
Induction		24.6	40.9	46.4 (not including planned CS)
Augmentation		47.4	72.1	64.8 (not including planned CS)
Episiotomy		19.1	82.2	n/a
Sutured		50.2	95.3	n/a
Continuous intrapartum monitoring		46.6	77.9	79.2 (not including planned CS)
Twins		1.5	3.9	8.9
Baby admitted to NNU		5.7	13.0	23.0

Table 2.11 Reasons given for having a caesarean section birth (more than one could be given)

Reported reasons for caesarean section	Planned CS N=210		Emergency CS N=204		All CS N=414	
	No.	%	No.	%	No.	%
Baby distressed	18	9	129	63	147	35
Baby in breech position	60	29	19	9	80	19
Twin pregnancy	23	11	12	6	35	8
Preterm labour	6	3	22	11	28	7
Maternal health	47	22	30	15	77	19
Previous CS	90	43	16	8	106	26
Labour failed to progress	7	3	97	48	104	25
Pelvic disproportion	48	23	48	24	96	23
I wished it that way	34	16	2	1	36	9
Other	32	15	20	10	52	13

'Other' reasons for caesarean section included a range of difficult presentations of the infant at delivery (12), placenta praevia (11), placental abruption (4), cord prolapse (3) and previous fetal death or stillbirth (5).

Table 2.12 Reported position at the time of giving birth (excluding CS births)

Reported position at delivery	No.	%
Lying flat on the bed	362	18
In stirrups lying on the bed	283	14
Sitting or propped up	1,143	58
Standing, squatting or kneeling	113	6
In a birthing pool	12	1
Other	55	3
Total	1,968	100

Table 2.13 Regional pattern of episiotomy (for all women having a vaginal delivery, N=1,919)

Region	Episiotomy No. of women	%
North	30	28
Yorks & Humberside	51	27
East Midlands	63	40
East Anglia	23	26
South East	195	28
South West	33	18
West Midlands	70	38
North West	55	26
Wales	19	19
Total episiotomy	539	

Table 2.14 Regional pattern of postnatal stay in hospital (N=2,309)

Region	<6 hours		6 to<24 hours		1-2 days		3-5 days		6 days or more	
	No.	%	No.	%	No.	%	No.	%	No.	%
North	3	2	19	15	32	25	61	48	13	10
Yorks & Humberside	7	3	47	21	77	34	72	32	23	10
East Midlands	9	5	30	16	54	29	70	38	21	11
East Anglia	2	2	25	23	34	32	37	35	9	8
South East	35	4	175	21	260	31	274	33	98	12
South West	7	3	39	18	60	27	82	37	33	15
West Midlands	4	2	40	18	71	32	80	36	27	12
North West	6	2	43	17	81	31	90	35	39	15
Wales	1	1	26	22	43	36	38	32	12	10

Table 2.15 Postnatal length of stay by type of delivery and for first time and other mothers

	First-time mothers			Other mothers		
	Normal vag.	Instr.	CS	Normal vag.	Instr.	CS
	%	%	%	%	%	%
Less than 6 hours	1	0	0	7	1	0
6 to <24 hours	6	4	0	37	18	<1
1-2 days	38	30	1	38	40	1
3-5 days	47	55	58	15	30	56
6 days or more	8	11	41	3	10	42
Total number of women	616	203	191	1,043	77	223

Table 2.16 Pattern of visits at home by a midwife up to the tenth day after the birth

	No.	%
	---	---
Visited every day up to 10 days	674	29
Visited every day except one	734	32
Visited every other day	671	29
Other	218	10
Total	2,297	100

Table 2.17 Age of baby at midwife's last visit

	No.	%
	---	---
Up to 10 days	1,014	45
11-15 days	763	34
16-28 days	409	18
More than 28 days	49	2
Total	2,235	100

Table 2.18 Regional pattern of age of baby at last visit of community midwife

Region	Stopped at 10 days or before		Stopped between 11 and 20 days		Stopped after 21 days	
	No.	%	No.	%	No.	%
North	44	39	58	51	12	11
Yorks & Humberside	77	37	96	46	38	18
East Midlands	92	51	65	36	24	13
East Anglia	41	40	38	37	24	23
South East	442	55	320	40	40	5
South West	97	45	104	48	15	7
West Midlands	86	42	102	50	18	9
North West	67	28	80	33	94	39
Wales	45	40	37	33	32	28
Total	991	100	900	100	297	100

Table 2.19 Percentages of women reporting problems among all those responding to the question (retrospective data)

Health problem:	10 days %	1 month %	3 months %
The blues	31	14	9
Continuing painful stitches	26	11	3
Breastfeeding problems	24	12	3
Depression	12	9	10
Wound infection	11	5 .	2
Losing urine when you don't mean to	13	9	4
Fatigue/ severe tiredness	43	31	21
Backache	35	27	28
Other	10	6	5
None of these (ticked)	18	34	45

Numbers:			
The blues	730	288	156
Continuing painful stitches	606	227	59
Breastfeeding problems	563	243	62
Depression	289	199	178
Wound infection	258	111	33
Losing urine when you don't mean to	317	180	91
Fatigue/ severe tiredness	1,015	645	385
Backache	836	559	516
Other	240	117	83
None of these (ticked)	437	727	829
Number answering	2,371	2,111	1,826
Question missed	35	295	580
Total	2,406	2,406	2,406

Note on Table 2.19: The responses to this question were hard to analyse. Although 99% of women answered the first part (about their health at ten days after the birth) the numbers responding fell off somewhat so that 88% answered about symptoms at one month and 76% for the three month part of the question. The question was probably quite demanding to answer because it required women to think back and remember how they had felt for a long list of symptoms. Women's recall may have been affected by their current state of health, and this cannot be allowed for in the analysis. It is also possible that women who missed the question were those who had no problems, but we do not have the means to check this within the dataset.

Table 2.20 During your pregnancy and around the time of the birth of your baby, was there anything that you felt you needed in the way of support or help that you didn't have? (could tick several options) (N=2,355)

	No. of mothers	%
More information from doctors	286	12
More information from midwives	236	10
Fewer different staff	428	18
More sympathetic medical care	197	8
More sympathetic midwifery care	191	8
More support from your partner	154	7
Other	62	3
I had all the support that I needed	1,462	62

Table 2.21 Perinatal factors as they relate to women whose babies were cared for in neonatal units, and differences between them and other mothers

Women whose babies were admitted to neonatal care:		NNU mothers No.	%		Other mothers No.	%
Were :	multips	122	56	} NS	1,175	57
	primip	97	44		875	43
Were aged:	15-24	57	26	} **	400	20
	25-34	121	55		1,370	67
	35-40+	42	19		282	14
Adverse obstetric history		65	30	NS	491	24
Had CVS or amniocentesis		23	11	**	113	6
Had antenatal checks:	low	100	48	} ***	587	30
	medium	70	34		911	46
	high	37	18		490	25
Had antenatal scans:	1-2	70	32	} ***	1,168	58
	3-4	82	37		622	31
	5 or more	67	31		242	12
Had predominantly hospital AN checks (H women)		43	21	***	257	13
Stayed in hospital antenatally for 3 nights or more		73	34	***	228	11
Had different types of delivery:	normal	92	42	} ***	1,508	74
	forceps	23	11		119	6
	ventouse	12	6		114	6
	caesarean section	93	43		311	15
Had a twin birth		40	18	***	33	2
Had a preterm infant (born at 37 weeks gestation or less)		123	57	***	94	8
Had a baby whose birthweight was <2,500g		97	44	***	60	3
Had a baby who was ventilated		68	31		not applicable	
Postnatal stays:	< 24 hours	4	2	} ***	492	24
	1-2 days	28	13		675	33
	3-5 days	74	34		723	35
	6 days or more	113	52		158	8

** significant at p<.01 level   *** significant at p<.001 level   NS not significant

Appendix 3 Studies of the views of maternity service users

Studies use a range of methods - postal surveys, interviews, observation of care and group discussions. Postal surveys are used the most, often with samples drawn from women using a maternity unit or from a local population of births. Some are carried out at a national level. For example, Ann Cartwright and her colleagues designed a survey to be used at national level. It was used in the early 1980s, and results were reported in a series of papers (Jacoby 1987, 1988; Jacoby and Cartwright 1990). The Infant Feeding Surveys are carried out for the government every five years by the Office for National Statistics (previously the Office of Population Censuses and Surveys) and questionnaires are sent to a national random sample of women who have recently had a birth (Foster et al, 1997).

In 1989 the Office of Population Censuses and Surveys published a manual for those carrying out maternity surveys (Mason 1989). The questionnaires included in this manual have been used widely in local surveys and also adapted recently (e.g. Lamping et al 1996; Hemingway et al 1994). A recent local study used a postal questionnaire and focus groups to explore some of the issues arising from *Changing Childbirth*. This was the Choices project which was carried out in Essex and was a collaboration between the National Childbirth Trust and purchasers (Gready et al, 1995).

Face-to-face interviews have been used in some cases rather than self administered questionnaires. These generally involve smaller samples, or greater cost, but allow topics to be covered in more depth. A classic early study in maternity by Ann Oakley used this method (eg, Oakley 1979, 1980). Studies of the views of Asian mothers (eg, Woollett and Dosanjh-Mattwala 1990; Rudat et al 1993; Bowes and Domokos, 1996) have been carried out using either interpreters or bi-lingual interviewers. Some studies in maternity have made use of observation of care, sometimes including interviews with those observed (eg, Kirkham, 1989; Garcia and Garforth, 1990; Hunt and Symonds, 1995). Focus groups have also been used; for example to allow a topic to be explored in more detail or to get information from women who are less likely to return questionnaires (eg, Gready et al, 1995).

Examples of studies using the range of methods, and further discussion about the advantages and disadvantages of each can be found in Garcia (1997). A conference report which deals with aspects of methodology but also covers ways of taking the views of service users into account is Dodds et al (1996). The College of Health is publishing a resource pack about methods of getting women's views in maternity care which will contain examples of questionnaires (Craig, 1998).

Appendix 4 **References**

References to relevant research and studies referred to in the report

Allen, I, Bourke Dowling, S, Williams, S (1997), *A Leading Role for Midwives*, London, Policy Studies Institute.

Barbour, R (1990), 'Fathers: the emergence of a new consumer group' in, Garcia, J, Kilpatrick, R, Richards, M (eds), *The Politics of Maternity Care*, Oxford, Oxford University Press.

Benbow, A, Semple, D, Maresh, M (1997), *Effective Procedures Suitable for Audit*, Manchester, Royal College of Obstetricians and Gynaecologists Clinical Audit Unit.

Bowes, A, Domokos, T (1996), 'Pakistani women and maternity care: raising muted voices' *Sociology of Health and Illness*, Vol. 18, pp 45-65.

Brown, S, Lumley, J, Small, R, Astbury, J (1994), *Missing Voices: the Experience of Motherhood*, Oxford, Oxford University Press.

Cartwright, A (1979), *The Dignity of Labour?*, London, Tavistock.

Cartwright, A (1983), *Health Surveys in Practice and Potential: A Critical Review of their Scope and Methods*, London, King Edward's Hospital Fund for London.

Cartwright, A (1986), 'Who responds to postal questionnaires?', *Journal of Epidemiology and Community Health*, Vol. 40, pp267-73.

Chamberlain, G, Wraight, A, Steer, P (1993), *Pain and its Relief in Childbirth*, Edinburgh, Churchill Livingstone.

Chamberlain, G, Wraight, A, Crowley, P (eds), (1996), *Home Births*, London, Parthenon Press.

Chapman, M, Roberts, E, Aherne, V, Harrison, A, Morgan, A (1996), *An Evaluation of Stockport Maternity Services*, Manchester, North West Surveys and Research.

Craig, G (1998), *Women's Views Count: Building Responsive Maternity Services*, London, College of Health.

Crombie, I, Davies, H (1996), *Research in Health Care: Design, Conduct and Interpretation of Health Services Research*, Chichester, John Wiley.

Department of Health, (1993), *Changing Childbirth*, London, HMSO.

Department of Health (1997), *NHS Maternity Statistics, England: 1989-90 to 1994-5*. Statistical Bulletin 1997/28, London, Department of Health.

Dodds, R, Goodman, M, Tyler, S (eds), (1996), *Listen with Mother: Consulting Users of Maternity Services*, Hale, Cheshire, Books for Midwives Press.

Farquhar, M, Camilleri-Ferrante, C, Todd, C (1996), *An Evaluation of Midwifery Teams in West Essex*. Cambridge, Public Health Resources Unit & Health Services Research Group, Institute of Public Health, University of Cambridge.

Foster, K, Lader, D, Cheesbrough, S (1997), *Infant Feeding 1995*, London, the Stationery Office.

Garcia, J, Garforth, S (1990), 'Parents and new-born babies in the labour ward' , in, Garcia, J, Richards, M, Kilpatrick, R (eds), *The Politics of Maternity Care*, Oxford, Oxford University Press.

Garcia, J, Renfrew, M, Marchant, S (1994), 'Postnatal home visiting by midwives', *Midwifery*, Vol. 10, pp40-3.

Garcia, J (1995), 'Continuity of carer in context: what matters to women?', in, Page, L (ed), *Effective Group Practice in Midwifery*, Oxford, Blackwell Scientific.

Garcia, J (1997), *Changing Midwifery Care: The Scope for Evaluation*, Oxford, National Perinatal Epidemiology Unit.

Gready, M, Newburn, M, Dodds, R, Gauge, S (1995), *Birth Choices: Women's Expectations and Experiences*, London, National Childbirth Trust.

Green. J, Coupland, V, Kitzinger, J (1990), 'Expectations, experiences and psychological outcomes of childbirth: a prospective study of 852 women', *Birth*, Vol. 17, pp15-24.

Green, J, Kitzinger, J, Coupland, V (1994), 'Midwives' responsibilities, medical staffing structures and women's choice in childbirth', in, Robinson, S, Thomson, A, (eds), *Midwives, Research and Childbirth*, Vol. 3, London, Chapman and Hall.

Hemingway, H, Saunders, D, Parsons, L (1994), *Women's Experiences of Maternity Services in East London: An Evaluation*, London, East London and City Health Authority.

Hunt, S, Symonds, A (1995), *The Social Meaning of Midwifery*, London, Macmillan.

Jacoby, A (1987), 'Women's preferences for and satisfaction with current procedures in childbirth - findings from a national study', *Midwifery*, Vol. 3, pp117-24.

Jacoby, A (1988), 'Mothers' view about information and advice in pregnancy and childbirth: findings from a national study', *Midwifery*, Vol. 4, pp103-10.

Jacoby, A, Cartwright, A (1990), 'Finding out about the views and experiences of maternity-service users', in, Garcia, J, Richards, M, Kilpatrick, R (eds), *The Politics of Maternity Care*, Oxford, Oxford University Press.

Kirkham, M (1983), 'Labouring in the dark - limitations on the giving of information to enable patients to orient themselves to the likely events and timescale of labour', in, Wilson-Barnett, J (ed), *Nursing Research: Ten Studies in Patient Care*, Chichester, John Wiley.

Kirkham, M (1989), 'Midwives and information-giving in labour', in, Robinson, S, Thomson, A (eds), *Midwives, Research and Childbirth*, Vol. I, London, Chapman and Hall.

Kitzinger, J, (1995), 'Introducing focus groups', *BMJ*, Vol. 311, pp299-302.

Lamping, D, Rowe, P (1996), *Surveys of Women's Experiences of Maternity Services (Short Form): Users' Manual for Purchasers and Providers*, London, London School of Hygiene and Tropical Medicine.

Leeds Family Health (1992), *Research into the Uptake of Maternity Services as Provided by Primary Health Care Teams to Women from Black and Ethnic Minorities*, Leeds, Leeds FSHA.

McCourt, C, Page, L (eds), (1996), *Report on the Evaluation of One-to-one Midwifery*, London, Thames Valley University and the Hammersmith Hospital NHS Trust.

McHaffie, H (1990), 'Mothers of very low birthweight babies: how do they adjust?' *Journal of Advanced Nursing*, Vol. 15, pp6-11.

McHaffie, H (1996), 'Supporting families with a very low birthweight baby' in Robinson, S, Thomson, A (eds), *Midwives, Research and Childbirth*, Vol. 4, London, Chapman and Hall.

McIntosh, J (1989) 'Models of childbirth and social class: a study of 80 working class primigravidae', in, Robinson, S, Thomson, A (eds), *Midwives Research and Childbirth*, Vol. 1, London, Chapman and Hall.

McIver, C (1994), *Obtaining the Views of Black Users of the Health Services*, London, King's Fund (copies from BEBC; for information freephone 0800-262260).

Martin, C (1987), 'Monitoring maternity services by postal questionnaire: congruity between mothers' reports and their obstetric records', *Statistics in Medicine*, Vol. 6, pp613-27.

Mason, V (1989), *Women's Experience of Maternity Care: A Survey Manual*, London, HMSO.

Mays, N, Pope, C (1996), *Qualitative Research in Health Care*, London, BMJ Publishing Group.

Mellor, J, Chambers, N (1995), 'Addressing the patient's agenda in the reorganisation of antenatal and infant health care: experience in one general practice', *British Journal of General Practice*, Vol. 45, pp423-5.

NHS Executive (1996), *Maternity Services Liaison Committees: Guidelines for Working Effectively*, Leeds, NHS Executive.

Oakley, A (1979), *Becoming a Mother*, Oxford, Martin Robertson.

Oakley, A (1980), *Women Confined: Towards a Sociology of Childbirth*, Oxford, Martin Robertson.

Oakley, A (1992), *Social Support and Motherhood*, Oxford, Blackwell.

Phoenix, A (1991), *Young Mothers?*, Cambridge, Polity Press.

Redshaw, M, Harris, A (1995), 'Maternal perceptions of neonatal care', *Acta Paediatrica Scandinavica*, Vol. 84, pp593-8.

Redshaw, M, Harris, A, Ingram, J (1996), *Delivering Neonatal Care: The Neonatal Unit as a Working Environment: A Survey of Neonatal Nursing*, London, HMSO.

Redshaw, M (1997), 'Mothers of babies requiring special care; attitudes and experiences', *Journal of Reproductive and Infant Psychology*, Vol. 15, pp109-20.

Renfrew, M J, Ross McGill, H (1996) *Enabling Women to Breastfeed: Interventions Which Support or Inhibit Breastfeeding - A Structured Review of the Evidence*. Leeds, Midwifery Studies, University of Leeds.

Royal College of Physicians (1988), *Medical Care of the Newborn in England and Wales*, London, Royal College of Physicians.

Rudat, K, Roberts, C, Chowdhury, R (1993), *Maternity Services: A Comparative Survey of Afro-Caribbean, Asian and White Women Commissioned by the Expert Maternity Group*, London, MORI Health Research.

Sikorski, J, Wilson, J, Clement, S, et al (1996), 'A randomised trial comparing two schedules of antenatal visits: the antenatal care project', *BMJ*, Vol. 312, pp546-53.

Woollett, A, Dosanjh-Matwala, N (1990), 'Postnatal care: the attitudes and experiences of Asian women in east London', *Midwifery*, Vol. 6, pp178-84.

Wray J (personal communication).